THE CHURCH AS EDUCATOR

CONRAD H. MOEHLMAN

Professor Emeritus, History of Christianity
The Colgate-Rochester Divinity School

HINDS, HAYDEN & ELDREDGE, Inc.

NEW YORK · PHILADELPHIA

Preface

For a millennium Christendom, the synthesis between the culture of Europe and Christianity, held sway in the western world. In the fifteenth century the powers of the modern age began to dissolve that synthesis. The totalitarian medieval religious structure was attacked from within by Protestantism and was further weakened by the invention of printing, the discovery of the Americas, the new astronomy, economic liberalism, religious toleration, political and religious liberty, denominationalism, sectarianism, and the cults. The power age brought large cities, industrialization, economic determinism, and science until the idea of "one world" cancelled out most of the medieval heritage.

For half a millennium Christendom had been disintegrating. Then came the San Francisco conference of 1945 ushering in a new age and demanding a new religious synthesis. Old things have passed away. Christianity's claim to uniqueness, often questioned in theory, faded before the facts at San Francisco. The meetings could not be opened with Christian prayers. It now became plain that all the believers in Christianity taken together constitute less than one-third of the earth's religious population. The "heathens" have been transformed into "co-members" of one world organization in which Confucianist, Buddhist, Hindu, Mohammedan, Jew, Christian, and innumerable other religious groups are getting ready to play their parts in the coming one-world symphony.

The old religious synthesis which spread throughout

Christian Europe is being replaced by an emerging synthesis where science will determine decisions. Gone are particular revelation and a peculiarly inspired Book and the disparagement of other peoples' experience of the Unknown. The trend is definitely toward a new life-synthesis in accord with the findings of science. Only two principal eras are discernible in the history of man: the era when religion was in the saddle, enduring in the western world to the sixteenth century; the era of transition since then to 1946, paving the way for the coming era of reconstruction and understanding.

The silence that hangs over the discussion of Christendom's guilt for the cataclysm which was the Europe of 1914–1945 is one of the amazing characteristics of contemporary history. For Fascism and Nazism demonstrated that Christendom was impotent to meet the problems of the new age. A Protestant researcher had noticed more than a quarter of a century ago that in southeastern Europe "the traditional Christian terminology was so absolutely identified with unchristian practices that to retain it would be like trying to discuss a color scheme with a man who is firmly convinced that red is blue and brown is green." A Catholic writing in these tragic times had pointed out that "the impotency and inadequacy of the forces of religion just at the time when they are most urgently needed is perhaps the most disheartening feature of the European situation today." The German pastor, "a fourth class salaried official, was regarded by some sections of the community as one of the black police; the growth of Social Democracy naturally increased anti-clericalism."

Let us consult the record. Christianity had been the religion of Europe for twelve centuries ere the decline of Christendom approached. Europe is the fatherland of modern war theory and methods and practice. Between 1815 and 1929, roughly from Napoleon to Hitler, there had been 252 wars there with 9 of great magnitude and 49 large-scale. The most Christian continent had been the most warlike and had transmitted its philosophy of war to the Americas and to the Orient.

Before Hitler rose to power, there were about 428 millions of Christians in Europe: 72 per cent, Catholic; 27 per cent, Protestant. Almost 98 out of every 100 Germans were inscribed members of the Christian churches. Germany, moreover, was the cradle of Protestantism. Hitler, Himmler, Goebbels, von Papen were Catholics; Goering, Hess, and Rosenberg were Protestants—Christians all! On Franklin D. Roosevelt's birthday in 1933, Hitler entered upon his dictatorship. Soon a concordat between Pius XI and Hitler was announced. Von Papen, papal chamberlain, hailed it thus: "The third Reich is the first power in the world not only to recognize but to translate into practice the high principles of the Papacy." He also proclaimed that Nazism was "the Christian countermovement against the spirit of 1789. . . . We, therefore, stand at the beginning of a Christian Revolution"! How meagre, too, were the efforts of the Christians of Germany, Europe, and the Americas against the introduction of racialism not only into German politics but also into the German churches. On October 18, 1945, the Council of the Protestant Church of Germany formally confessed its guilt in a declaration stating: ". . . We know ourselves to be one with our people in a great company of suffering, but also in a great solidarity of guilt. With great pain do we say: through us has endless suffering been brought to many peoples and countries. . . ."

The Treysa Conference of the new "Evangelical Church of Germany" also stated: "Long before the sham government of our land broke down, justice had been thwarted. Long before men were murdered, men had become mere ciphers, and for this reason of no worth. When a man's life becomes worthless, he thinks nothing of taking human life."

Listen next to Niemoeller: "If the church 'had seen clearly and acted unitedly, this terrible war never would have arisen' "—quite a transformed Niemoeller!

The Axis Powers have been defeated and with them Europe. The religious synthesis which was the culture of Europe combined with ecclesiastical Christianity has come to its twilight, for, as that able Catholic writer, Hilaire Belloc, says: "Europe is the Faith, and the Faith is Europe." But the new synthesis forming during the transition period is ready to take over. The beginning in the politico-economic area appeared at San Francisco. Religion must follow.

This study is designed to put the religious phase of the breakdown of the medieval religious synthesis and the birth of the modern religious synthesis in proper perspective. It examines in broad outline that breakdown, paying special attention to four major trends: racialism, the evangelization of the world in this generation, the failure of two attempts to compromise, namely, the American social gospel and religious education.

Dealing, thereupon, with the American landscape, it shows how the new synthesis has won the war in American education against ecclesiastical reaction in both the university and public school areas. The released time experiment is seen to be the final feeble attempt of ecclesiastical ignorance to guide the American way of life.

The third section of the analysis is concerned with various suggestions looking toward a formulation of the new synthesis in practical terms. It gives particular emphasis to four necessary understandings of the new tasks facing the churches.

CONTENTS

To

HORACE M. KALLEN

and

WILLIAM H. KILPATRICK

Who Expanded My Horizons

AN AMERICAN EDUCATION FELLOWSHIP BOOK

Part One

*The Disintegration of the Inherited
Western Religious Synthesis*

Chapter One

The Twilight of the Gods

Christianity originated within Judaism. To this day the deposit of that religion in all types of Christianity is considerable.

Jesus of Nazareth was a Jew born of Jewish parents on Jewish soil within the Jewish tradition. He never lived beyond the Jewish homeland, never visited the great cities of the Graeco-Roman world. In a few miles of the Mediterranean area, known as Palestine, he was born, lived, and died. His people's Bible, now called the Old Testament, was his Bible. His religious pronouncements, the very words in which he clothed them, are found in the earlier and contemporary sayings of Judaism. When he formulated his creed, he merely combined Deuteronomy 6:5 and Leviticus 19:18, obtaining "And thou shalt love the Lord thy God with all thine heart, and with all thy soul, and with all thy might; thou shalt love thy neighbor as thyself." The petitions of the prayer ascribed to him and now recited in Christian churches the world over are found in earlier Jewish prayers. The personality of Jesus bears the ineffaceable impression of his Jewish inheritance.

The original glowing faith of the followers of Jesus was the hope of the immediate, supernatural, cataclysmic establishment of the overworldly kingdom of God upon this earth. In this paradise his disciples would fully enjoy God. During the brief interim prior to the visible descent of the

Master upon the clouds of the sky, they intended to live in complete separation from the evil world all about them. They made no blueprint of ecclesiastical organization; they never dreamed of apostolic succession; they never produced a Bible of their own but derived all their religion from the Bible of their people and the sayings of Jesus; they never fashioned the so-called apostles' creed. Why should they? Within a generation there was not going to be any evil world.

But Jesus did not descend upon the clouds of heaven to judge the world in one grand court scene. Their atomic bomb which was utterly to destroy the existing world never exploded. Hence, about the time of the destruction of Jerusalem in A.D. 70, this original faith collapsed. The faith upon which original Christianity rested vanished. Its reconstruction began and has been going on ever since. Allegorized, symbolized, transformed into something or other it never had been, the original Christian faith has survived in ever new rationalizations to the present moment. The pressure of the nineteenth-century social order upon intelligent Christians persuaded them to turn the original overworldly kingdom of God into organic process more consonant with modern developmental theories, but this "social gospel" also failed.

The cradle of the new faith was Asia. Christianity by its ancestry seemed destined to be an Oriental religion. But it has never appealed to the continent of its birth. Within four decades the Christian mother church at Jerusalem had lost control over the numerous mission stations. In Samaria, the east Jordan region, Arabia, the Tigris-Euphrates valley, Syria, and Asia Minor, the advance of the new religion was retarded. In later times, the crusades failed. The modern Mohammedan world is a tough field for Christian missionaries.

Defeated in Asia, Christianity responded to the need of

Macedonia. Moving along the Hellenized coast of Phoenicia and Syria, first north, then west, it finally entered Europe from Troas. Rome would become its capital, and Europe its destiny. Only now did the Roman empire discern its blunder in identifying Christianity with Judaism. From Nero's day to the reign of Constantine, Christianity was an unrecognized religion. Because it was politically expedient, Constantine granted Christianity legal recognition. Within three-quarters of a century, it became the imperial religion.

Sheltered for three decades through its identification with Judaism by the Roman Empire, the new religion had the necessary time to penetrate to the great centres of that empire before it was outlawed. The secret meetings of the Christians and particularly the manner of celebrating the Lord's Supper caused the citizens of the Roman Empire to accuse them of engaging in "Thyestic feasts and Oedipodic unions." It was alleged that Christians initiated their young novices by the sacrifice of an infant covered with meal and that at their communion services they became thoroughly intoxicated, engaging in incest "in the shameless darkness." Falsely charged with having set Rome on fire, they served as nocturnal torches. Because they refused to buy meat sacrificed to idols, books of magic, statuettes of the goddess Diana, and to worship the divine Emperor, and because they invited sinners to their meetings, Christians until the fourth century were classified as unpatriotic and guilty of treason.

Toward the end of that century, *Christianity, hitherto only a religion, became a new thing, namely, Christendom, by fusion with the culture of the Roman Empire*. It was the "one-world" thinking of that day. One society for Europe captured the imagination as the decades came and went. The old *respublica* became *respublica Christiana*, the city of God. Practically speaking, the Eastern Empire did not become a member; there were Jewish communities in Europe excluded from membership; Moorish power and civilization refused to be absorbed; and pockets of paganism persisted.

Christianity was formally and externally amalgamated with Graeco-Roman civilization after four centuries of separateness, but actually the process was on from Paul's day—thus early was the ethical religion of Jesus turned into a theology of a dying and rising Savior. Gradually the gospel concerning Jesus absorbed the magic, mythology, folklore, and philosophy of Europe. The people's faith was never that of the hierarchy. "Church history" magnifies doctrine and organization and ecclesiasticism and thus far has done little to uncover the social and religious elements of the people's Christianity.

Studied as creed, episcopate, canonization of the New Testament, rise of the papacy, and monasticism, church history is misleading. Christianity cannot be pried loose from Europe. Constantine the Emperor presided at meetings of the Council of Nicaea as "equal to the apostles." The king was the Lord's anointed and therefore sacred. His anointing was a sacrament, *making him a sacred person*, for he then received the Holy Spirit. In England, His Majesty still claims the tithe as due him. Separation of church and state must be tolerated by the church today but it can never be approved by it.

Christendom, *defined as Europe's civilization and religion*, signified an international church, an *imperium*, a *sacerdotium*, a society composed of the minority of the perfect who did more than was required for salvation and the majority who could not, the power over death in the anathema and the power over life in the sacrament. Christendom meant control over the economic life, marriage, and the home and education, with just price, just wars, social need restricting money-making, production subordinated to consumption, suffering as punishment for sin, but above all and conditioning all—submission to authority. Revelation and authority were the twin problem-solvers. Original sin was

always available as the scapegoat for any emergency. Since
the doctrine of the virgin birth did nothing about the passage of original sin from the body of Mary into that of
Jesus, the doctrine of the immaculate conception of Mary
in the womb of her mother had to be added. Disease was of
divine sending. Woman was degraded into a witch and de-
bates were staged as to whether or not she was a human
being at all. The earth was an enlarged pancake at peace and
rest, not rotating upon its own axis or revolving around a
central sun; rather, the sun sank nightly in the west to be
ferried back to the east in a boat rowed on an underearth
river where it would arrive in time to dawn at the right
moment.

Glance at a chart of Christendom as compared with a
chart of modern culture. In the former there are great open
spaces, seldom occupied, in all the branches of science—it
is the religious age. In the latter, all the areas of science are
securely held and overcrowded, with organized religion
making few creative suggestions to aid science in interpreting the bewildering discoveries of the transition to 1946.
Someone has counted the contributions made to civilization between 1775 and 1928: 66 by science, 7 by law, 6 by
religion; and a pre-eminent modern scientist has said: "Since
the rise of modern science, no decided change or striking forward advance has been made by religion."

If in 1517 any European Christian had foretold that four
centuries later the one and only church would have been
broken up into more than 350 fragments in the United
States alone he might have been haled before some inquisi-
torial court. But that could not have prevented the five
huge waves of the future from rolling in and bringing Christendom to its period of decline.

The first wave that began to undermine the foundations
of Christendom rolled in between 1450 and 1650 for two
long centuries. Its religious deposit was the emergence and

establishment of Protestantism, the beginning of secularization, the end of the universal church. About 1840, Orestes Brownson, later a convert to Catholicism, wrote: ". . . At the epoch of the Reformation [the Catholic Church] had finished its work, fulfilled its mission, and since then it has been a mere cumberer of the ground."

The second wave of the transition to the contemporary age rose higher but was of less duration than the first, 1650–1791. On the religious side its deposit was surrender of control of marriage, education, and the economic life to the state and the achievement of religious and political liberty in the United States. Its greatest damage to what had been was to be the revolutionary view that political power derives from the people who elect their ruler rather than accept him from God.

The third wave that permanently injured Christendom was little more than a century in duration, 1791–1899. Its deposit was the shift in civilization from the muscle of the individual to the power stored up in the machine. It ushered in modern science and historical method and industrialization and the developmental hypothesis.

The fourth wave that followed so mercilessly lasted for less than half a century, 1899 to 1945, but was much more violent and destructive in its religious deposit. For history of religions, the psychological approach to religion, modern racialism, two world wars, Nazism, and similar factors have made Christendom obsolete and the rethinking of Christianity itself essential.

And then the fifth wave of the future rolled in upon a sorrowful earth in 1945. Will it have dissipated its strength by 1965? It was set in motion by the defeat of the Axis Powers, the adoption of the United Nations Charter at San Francisco, the ratification of that Charter by the Senate of the United States, and the discovery and manufacture and dropping of atomic bombs upon cities in Japan. It may lead either to the unity of man or to the disappearance of man from the face of the earth.

The first wave of the future was started on its way when printing from movable type destroyed the aristocracy of education. Then followed other influences which weakened the hold of the church hierarchy over the masses. Their faith in the geography of the Bible was shaken when one of Magellan's ships succeeded in sailing around the world. The flat earth, six parts land and one part water according to the medieval Bible, became a rotating and revolving sphere and condemned several verses of the Bible to oblivion. Science marched onward. Telescope and microscope challenged the received dogmas of Christianity. Illness was no longer attributed to inner devils but to bacteria first seen through his microscope by Antony van Leeuwenhoek in the seventeenth century. The progress of science weakened the authority of the papacy and advanced the struggle for the rights of man.

Protestantism merely represented the religious phase of the movement toward the rights of man. It divided the one and only sound church into hundreds of confident sects forever in schism and in error. Protestantism, however, failed to discard the luggage bequeathed it by the medieval church. It continued to be sacramental and institutional in emphasis when the new age was demanding a return to the originally ethical emphases of the Judaeo-Christian heritage. By mid-seventeenth century Protestantism consisted of a group of static churches, each protected by its "secure" confessional wall, but each also incapable of adapting itself to and interpreting the new civilization. What had been Christendom began to dissolve.

All this contradictory European Protestantism—Anglicanism, Congregationalism, Baptists, Quakers, Presbyterians, Reformed, Lutherans, Moravians, Dunkers, Mennonites, French Protestants, Sandemanians, Methodists, and all the others—the second wave of the future then deposited in the British colonies in North America, with Anglicanism solidly occupying the southern colonies; Congregationalism, New England; but with many sects in the middle colonies, their differences guaranteeing tolerance and, at last, religious liberty. For, in the strange ever-changing American environment, new ideas continuously appeared and the dogmas of the various confessions of faith could not be enforced.

The pale religious toleration act of 1689 released the hitherto directed English religious intellect, and Deism annihilated beyond recognition *credo quia absurdum*. The contents of the Bible were laid bare and dissected. The other than Christian religions of the East were studied and hidden defects of Christianity came to light. Common sense was entered as a factor in religious discussion. Opposition to dogmas of religion spread among many of the leaders in the American Revolution, and one of the Founding Fathers remarked that "this would be the best of all possible worlds, if there were no religion in it." Just as at the convening of the United Nations at San Francisco, the meetings of the committee framing the Constitution of the United States were not opened with prayer.

Jonathan Edwards preached hell-fire. Who today can read his "sinners in the hands of an angry God" without shuddering? But his rejection of the halfway covenant and the failure of his revival and his emphasis on individual experience in religion helped New England liberalism. The rise of Universalism among the disciples of Calvinist Whitefield indicates how Calvinism itself demands the salvation of all men after affirming the damnation of most. "As in Adam *all die*, so in Christ shall *all be made alive*." It is the identical "all." Unitarianism, much more radical than its sister denomination, made it unnecessary for "those born in Boston to be born again."

American Protestantism fought on the side of the revolutionists and for Amendment I and Article VI. Europe knew that the new government was different from what had been. The concept of Christendom is in basic disagreement with the American way of life. As an American historian pointed out in 1823: "The government of the United States seems to be without a parallel. We find nothing like it in modern times. . . . Our government is no less singular as to its nature than as to its origin. . . . In our case, a number of men competent to so great a work sat down and planned our government. Before them lay the legislation of past ages. . . . The plan they formed was dictated by their knowledge of our circumstances; and it is probably the ablest and best plan of government ever formed by man." It did not come by revelation but by research. It was based not upon Romans 13 but upon history. It set aside the political postulates of Christendom and substituted those of the rights of man.

The religious quadrilateral of the American way is:

1. 1787, "An ordinance for the government of the territory of the United States, northwest of the Ohio River. Article I. No person, demeaning himself in a peaceful and orderly manner shall ever be molested on account of his mode of worship or religious sentiments, in the said Territory. . . . Article VI. There shall be neither slavery nor involuntary servitude in said Territory. . . ."

2. 1787, Article VI, Constitution of the United States, ". . . but no religious test shall ever be required as a qualification to any office or public trust under the United States."

3. 1791, Amendment I, "Congress shall make no law respecting an establishment of religion, or prohibiting the free exercise thereof."

4. 1791, Amendment V, "No person shall be . . . deprived of life, liberty, or property, without due process of law."

The "shift in civilization," the transfer from the energy in the muscle of man to the duplicating power of the machine, began with Watt's steam engine, 1775, and has now gone beyond the atom-smashing phase. Between 1850 and 1900, we are informed by S. S. Wyer, inventions and discoveries came to sixty times as many as between 1450 and 1500. Between 1920 and 1930 the United States patent office considered seventy-one times as many claims as between 1840 and 1850. In 1929 there was eighty-four times as much horsepower in use as in 1869. The twentieth century accepts all verifiable findings of science whether they agree with or violently contradict the assumptions of religion. Fear and authority and mystery are vanishing—intelligence replacing ignorance and courage conquering fear. The grandeur of man is being established daily in thousands of research laboratories. Man is learning how to control his environment and fashion his future, and his religion undergoes corresponding transformations. The principle of the separation of church and state will some day be accepted the world over. Universal free public education is no longer an ideal but is coming to pass. Science can no longer be halted by religious anathemas. The developmental hypothesis is accepted in all areas beyond that of religion.

Despite all sectarian opposition the Bible has become an historical book. The heretics know that it required centuries for the "books of Moses" to grow into their traditional form and have revised the spelling of Pentateuch into JEDP.* Isaiah is a product of the eighth to second centuries before the common era. The first page of Genesis and the last page of Malachi were written in the same century. The Psalter was not completed until the period of the Maccabean revolution in the second century. Job could not have been composed until the suffering of the righteous

---

* Jahvist, Elohistic, Deuteronomic, priestly codes now used in the study of the Old Testament.

individual had become a problem for Israel in the Greek period. The text of the King James Version, based upon a few late cursives, has surrendered to that found in the Revision, in Moffatt, in Goodspeed. The authorized confraternity edition of the Douay version again and again accepts alterations of the text of the New Testament—a procedure which would have involved ecclesiastical discipline in the nineteenth century. The so-called centuries of silence between the close of the Old Testament and the beginning of the New Testament have become vocal with scores of significant literary compositions. In the New Testament are direct quotes and echoes from Old Testament and "inter-Biblical" thinking. The writers of the New Testament knew only the Old Testament as an inspired volume. In a word, the Bible of yesterday and that of the historian are incommensurable.

During the machine age, labor deserted the churches to such an extent that Pius XI lamented, "The great scandal of the nineteenth century was that the Church lost the laboring class." The Vatican, rejecting the trends of nineteenth-century Europe, abandoned its policy of isolationism only in the days of Leo XIII who accepted conciliation in *Rerum Novarum*. The rise of the theory of economic determinism and also that of organic development disturbed the churches grievously but could not be uprooted. In the 1880's learned Christian theologians might still oppose the establishment of history of religions chairs in universities and divinity schools because only Christianity was a revealed religion. Today Christianity must be studied as any other religion and its agreements with the religions of the world admitted.

Dwight L. Moody, the last of the great American evangelists, died in 1899. In that year, Starbuck published his *Psychology of Religion* which invaded the realm of the soul and questioned the theological interpretation of conversion.

"One of the forces working in revivals is that of suggestion and hypnotism," wrote he. What then remained of "the birth from above," "regeneration," "the mystery of conversion," John 3:3–8? Within a few years, regeneration became "religious committal"—an act of God in the soul of man was demoted to an act of man in deciding to join a church. Formerly the call to the Christian ministry had been viewed as a summons to preach original sin and guilt by one who had himself experienced its removal. Now the dogma cannot be found in the Old Testament or the New Testament by historians nor in psychology by the successors of Starbuck. About 1910 the young candidates for the ministry remembered only that they had been born in Christian homes.

In 1902 William James published *Varieties of Religious Experience, A Study in Human Nature.* Religious men hailed the conclusions of the Harvard professor who "thought religion worthy of his laborious attention." Religion was returning in grand style to the Harvard curriculum! The volume rapidly went through twenty-six printings. Alas, it was belatedly observed that James of Harvard had returned not to Paul whose thinking was regarded as the basis of Protestantism but to James of the New Testament whose ethics Martin Luther had frowned upon. Jonathan Edwards had been naturalized, and conversion located "within the frontiers of the human personality." The traditional supernatural intervention to save man from hell yielded to Christian nurture and religious education. After that, psychoanalysis explained Moses, Isaiah, Jesus, Paul, and St. Francis of Assisi without resort to the old dogmas.

Methodist pietism was a principal trend in nineteenth-century American Christianity. In the twentieth century a Methodist minister's son published *Your City* and concluded that the church as an institution "has little, if any, measurable influence upon the good life in any community.

. . . The correlation of church membership with the good life may be negative."

The conflict between the Christian tradition and the practical faith and activity of the twentieth-century man is so serious that the Christian lives continuously in two contradictory worlds. Can the inherited faith be synthesized with his contemporary conduct? Can the "integration and cooperation between man's beliefs about the world in which he lives and his beliefs about the values and purposes that should direct his conduct" be restored? Shall the chaos which is Europe spread to all the earth because religion insists upon lagging behind science and thereupon blames the scientist for creating confusion?

The Christendom which was the synthesis of Europe's civilization and Christianity declined because it refused to be ethicized, to take the Golden Rule and the summary of Jesus out of its museum of relics. Instead, it sought to secure its objectives by influencing or controlling the state. It reduced the grandeur of man to zero and was unconcerned about the contemporary needs of the people. It called social Christianity mere "activism" and permitted *Volksreligion* to be directed against Judaism. Christendom tolerated outrage after outrage against the rights of man until it was too late, and Nazism's reign of terror was in full swing. Genuine peace will not return to Europe until its remnants of Christianity not only repent at the altar but also put ethical practice above dogma in life. The experience of the churches of Europe is a clarion call to Christian groups everywhere to the reaffirmation and the practice of ethical religion.

In the Norse mythology the souls of the slain were carried to Valhalla, abode of the immortals, by the valkyr. The final destruction of the existing world-order resulted from the strife between the gods and the powers of Hel. The twilight of the gods terminated their age-long struggle with the giants. Both giants and the good gods perished in mutual annihilation. But that was not the end of things. A new earth without the gods appeared, for Fate was superior to the gods. The gods had arranged, ruled, and protected the existing world-order and courageously fought against its disappearance; all in vain! The old gods died with the world-order of their creation. Can men become brothers in this twentieth century only through the death of the faiths which have made them enemies?

Richard Wagner's *Twilight of the Gods* has two endings. In the earlier the comely valkyr announces:

> The race of gods is vanished like a breath
> And masterless I leave the world behind.

Wagner then accepted the Judaeo-Christian tradition and joyously let the maiden grant man a more than equivalent substitute for the gods: Love—on the basis of brotherhood a better world-order shall arise.

But Wagner later turned pessimist. The optimism of Judaism and of Christianity gave way to the pessimism of Buddhism. Gone were hope and brotherhood and the better world-order. A second ending was composed. The valkyr now bequeathed to man, creator of will and idea, of desire and delusion and "eternal oscillation," only endless pain and misery until the neutrality which is Nirvana is attained.

In England the coming synthesis, rejecting Wagner's pessimism, was thus expounded in *Joshua Davidson*: "I have proved to myself the whole meaning of Christ; it is Humanity. The modern Christ . . . would accept the truths of science and he would teach that a man saves his own soul by helping his neighbour. . . ."

In the United States the religion that matters is in practice discarding or at least disregarding the dogmas that bind it to past errors and slowly gaining in competency not only to live in harmony with the scientific way of life but also to think according to the newer assumptions.

In Revelation 21, one reads: "And I saw the holy city, new Jerusalem, coming down from God out of heaven . . . AND A TEMPLE I SAW NOT IN IT." "Two very startling things arrest our attention," writes Henry Drummond, fellow worker of the great American evangelist, Dwight L. Moody, "in John's vision of the future. The first is that the likest thing to heaven he could think of was a City; the second, that there was no Church in that City"— city "the antipodes of heaven"; no church, the "defiance of all religion."

"Believe me," countered Jesus, "a time approaches when it will be neither upon this mount nor in Jerusalem that you will worship the Father. . . . God is spirit; those who worship him must worship spiritually and sincerely."

Chapter Two

That Man Gobineau

The Judaeo-Christian literature contains beautiful passages on human brotherhood. Malachi 2:10 makes its basis religious: "Have we not all one Father? Hath not one God created us?" Micah 4:4 anticipates a time of peace and security: "But they shall sit every man under his vine and under his fig tree; and none shall make them afraid." Leviticus 19:18 makes justifiable love of self the measure of attitude toward fellow man: "Thou shalt love thy neighbor as thou shalt love thyself." Jesus regards the practice of neighborliness the test of the good neighbor in Luke 10:36. Acts 17:26 affirms the common origin of all nations: "All nations he has created from a common origin." Whoever inserted the marginal note which became Romans 2:14, 15 profoundly felt that human differences are man-made.

But the practice of brotherhood in Christendom is another matter. Three examples of man's inhumanity to man are found in the Christian treatment of woman, the Negro, and the Jew. The Fascist, repudiating democracy and the working classes, also opposed the emancipation of woman, confining her to *Kueche, Kinder, Kirche*. He condemned the Negro to the lowest rank in the racial scale and the Jew to eradication. But he was nourished on what Christendom had said about and done to woman and Negro and Jew. Only occasionally does a Cotton Mather appear who in his

Essays To Do Good so violently criticized slavery that the American Tract Society expurgated the text.

The annual importation of shanghaied African slaves into the Protestant colonies in North America early in the eighteenth century amounted to 25,000. By 1771 this number had been doubled. The planters opposed the Christianization of the Negro because he did not know English, would be less governable, did not like Christianity, was stupid, and would have to be more mercifully treated. Conversion to Christianity did not alter slave status but was only deliverance from sin and Satan.

Evangelist Whitefield helped introduce slavery into Georgia contrary to the desire of the colonists and died holder of seventy-five slaves. Here is his argument in behalf of Negro slavery:

As to the lawfulness of keeping slaves, I have no doubt since I hear of some that were bought with Abraham's money, and some that were born in his house. I, also, cannot help thinking, that some of those servants mentioned by the Apostles, in their epistles, were or had been slaves. It is plain that the Gideonites were doomed to perpetual slavery; and though liberty is a sweet thing to such as are born free, yet to those who never knew the sweets of it, slavery perhaps may not be so irksome.

However this may be, it is plain to a demonstration, that hot countries cannot be cultivated without Negroes. What a flourishing country might Georgia have been, had the use of them been permitted years ago. How many white people have been destroyed for want of them and how many thousands of pounds spent to no purpose at all. Had Mr. Henry been in America, I believe he would have seen the lawfulness and necessity of having Negroes there. And, though it is true that they are brought in a wrong way from their native country, and it is a trade not to be approved of, yet, as it will be carried on whether we will or not, I should think myself highly favored if I could purchase a good number of them, to make their lives comfortable, and lay a foundation for breeding up their posterity in the nurture and admonition of the Lord.

You know, dear sir, that I had no hand in bringing them into Georgia. Though *my judgment was for it*, and so much money was yearly spent to no purpose and I was strongly importuned thereto, yet I would have no Negro upon my plantation till the use of them was publicly allowed in the colony. Now this is done, let us reason no more about it, but diligently improve the present opportunity for their instruction.

An ordinance for the government of the territory of the United States northwest of Ohio River, 1787, prohibited slavery in Article VI. But section 9 of Article I of the Constitution of the United States permitted the importation of slaves at a head tax of no more than ten dollars until 1808, and paragraph 3 of section 2 of Article IV ensured the return of runaway slaves. The invention of the cotton gin made slavery profitable by multiplying the individual slave's capacity one hundred fold. Economic forces intensified the slavery issue.

As the slavery issue became acute various Protestant denominations suffered schism; Friends, Baptists, Presbyterians, Methodists.

Armstrong's *The Christian Doctrine of Slavery* argued that according to the scriptural theory of the origin of slavery, degradation is the effect of sin for both nations and individuals. Slavery is punitive and remedial. The second degree of slavery is subjection to a despotic government, and the third degree is personal or chattel slavery. Neither Christ nor his apostles regarded slave-holding as a sin. The numerous sin-catalogues in the New Testament fail to mention slavery. All the New Testament books were written in slave-holding states and addressed to persons and churches in slave-holding states. The condition of slaves in Judea was the condition of slaves in our southern states. Christ and his apostles acknowledged the existence of slavery. The apostles welcomed slaveholders into their churches. Paul sent a fugitive slave back to his master. Paul repeatedly enjoined their respective duties upon masters and slaves. Paul declared his doctrine wholesome and treated the distinctions which slavery created as matters of trivial significance. Paul directed Christian ministers to teach the Biblical doctrine respecting the duties of slaves. The rights of the master were obedience and service. The rights of the slave were "that which is just and equal." Slaves must be admitted to membership in Christian churches, where there is neither bond nor free.

In *The American Churches, the Bulwarks of American Slavery, the Commencement of the Christian Dispensation,* and *The Brotherhood of Thieves, or a True Picture of the American Church and Clergy,* indictments of Protestant attitudes toward Negro slavery appear in great quantity. James G. Birney, the author of the first of the three tracts, was a native of Kentucky and a slaveholder who met Theodore D. Weld, a principal propagandist for the abolition of slavery. Converted to the antislavery view, Birney emancipated his forty-two slaves and was driven from Kentucky for antislavery activity. In Ohio he established an antislavery newspaper, whose presses were sunk in the Ohio River. His very popular tract was a sharp attack upon the Protestant churches. Its accusations, a century after, still blister. Methodists, Baptists, Presbyterians, and Episcopalians are summoned for arraignment and judgment.

This attack upon the Protestant churches for their share in the maintenance of Negro slavery in the United States has been softened by the recent study of the career of Theodore Dwight Weld, a convert of Evangelist Charles G. Finney. As the second president of Oberlin College, Finney persuaded students to support the abolition cause and influenced Garrison. He aroused the rural towns and villages, enlisting Presbyterians, Methodists, and Baptists in the antislavery crusade. These with the Congregationalists participated actively in the fight for freedom. But the campaign of these comparatively few rebels within the church collapsed because of the rise of sectionalism, the Biblicism in the Protestant churches, and the trend toward political action. "The most pathetic residue of the anti-slavery organization was the little group which had attempted to turn the anti-slavery impulse toward political action. In 1840, they organized the Liberty Party and nominated J. G. Birney for president, but among the millions who cast their ballots in the national election they won him barely 7,000 votes." Between 1842 and 1844 Weld turned lobbyist and brought the antislavery impulse to the Congress of the United States. For him and his supporters, slavery was a moral and religious, not an economic issue. Material advantages for the North did not summon northern ministers, merchants, mechanics, or farmers to the fray.

Despite the unworthy record of the mass of church members, on the slavery question, a brave minority kept up the good fight. Indeed, two-thirds of those participating in the organization of the American Antislavery Society were church members and three-fourths of the antislavery agents and editors were clergymen. Oliver Johnson later acknowledged that the "anti-slavery movement originated in the deepest religious convictions and derived its main impulse from the spirit of Christianity in the hearts of its champions." And Garrison himself maintained that "his converts were most likely to be made among those whose consciences had been educated by the church and the Bible."

Moreover, a recently recovered address by Lincoln, of

May 6, 1842, reveals the emancipator as a pioneer aboli-
tionist who supported the position of the church minority:

> In what I have done, I cannot claim to have acted from
> any peculiar consideration of the colored people as a sepa-
> rate and distinct class in the community, but from the
> simple conviction that all the individuals of that class
> in the community are members of the community, and,
> in virtue of their manhood, entitled to every original
> right enjoyed by any other member. We feel, therefore,
> that all legal distinctions between individuals of the
> same community founded on any such circumstances as
> color, origin, and the like, are hostile to the genius of our
> institutions, and incompatible with the true history of
> American liberty. Slavery and oppression must cease, or
> American liberty must perish. True democracy makes no
> inquiry about the color of the skin, or the place of nativ-
> ity, or any other similar circumstances of condition.

Recent historical study has shown that American Catholic attitude toward the Negro slave paralleled that of the
inactive mass of Protestantism. Archbishop Hughes of New
York judged that the American Negro slavery system had
the consent of God. In the dogma of the church, slavery was
interpreted as a consequence of original sin, applying particularly to the descendants of Ham. In his letter to the
Secretary of War, Hughes wrote: "The Catholics, so far as I
know, whether of native or foreign birth, are willing to
fight to the death for the support of the Constitution, the
Government, and the laws of the country. But if it should
be understood that, with or without knowing it, they are
to fight for the abolition of slavery, then, indeed, they will
turn away in disgust from the discharge of what would
otherwise be a patriotic duty." Few Catholics supported the
abolition movement in any form. Chief Justice Taney, a
Catholic, rendered the Dred Scott decision. Abraham Lin-

coln, thereupon, delivered his "divided house" speech. During the Civil War, northern Roman Catholics tended to go with the Union, while those in the South supported states' rights.

Christendom's inability to practice its racial ideals is dramatically illustrated by the *Volksreligion* of Germany during the last century. Fascism as an economic structure rests in part upon the ideas of the Frenchman Proudhon and as a racial theory upon the assertions of the Frenchman Gobineau. Neither of these Frenchmen was approved by the French. But they gave the push-off to the twin evils of Nazi totalitarianism: Fascism and anti-Semitism. For three-quarters of a century Nazism's racialism was in the making while the Christian churches slept on. *Mein Kampf* was consummation, not beginning.

Volksreligion went romantic and nationalistic before accepting racialism. Had not Hegel proclaimed that "the State is the divine idea as it exists on earth. . . . All the worth which the human being possesses, all spiritual reality, he possesses only through the State"? Then it turned to Gobineau.

Joseph Arthur Gobineau is written up in the Nazi lexicons. He was a French writer, we are told, who made a basic contribution to the "doctrine of the races of man" by suggesting the "Aryan idea"! His treatise upon the inequality of the human races profoundly influenced Wagner, Nietzsche, and Chamberlain. Written in the 1850's from a conservative Catholic point of view as a polemic against the European swing toward democracy, and definitely pro-Nordic, the essay was a poor seller in France. Popularized by Richard Wagner and his circle in Bayreuth, its ideas paved the way for Nazism.

Gobineau held that the three primary races are the yellow, the white, and the black, permanently unequal and forever different in cultural capacity. The white race is the highest in the scale, and the Germans lead the white procession. In cultural creativity the Germans have no superior and no equal. All racial mixture is deteriorating. The contemporary European decadence has resulted from the passing of the old families, the rise of the middle class, and the rise of the proletariat. A lower race cannot rise but is condemned to remain forever in its present status. The amount of Nordic blood in any people determines its rank in the racial hierarchy. European civilization began with the German invasions. Ancestor worship should be cultivated because it preserves racial purity and capacity to govern. Accepting whole-heartedly these fallacies of race-theory, *Volksreligion* took a short cut toward Fuehrer Adolf and smooth Herr Rosenberg. Between 1910 and 1920 Schemann published six volumes on Gobineau and founded the Gobineau Association.

Upon the journey thither Lagarde, born Boetticher, is met. Orientalist, political writer in behalf of a greater Germany and a national church, he desired a German church "which would not only surmount confessional differences but also find room for vital elements in German paganism." He appreciated neither Lutheranism nor Protestantism. His "German Christianity" excluded the Judaeo-Christian tradition. This compelled him to become an anti-Semite, and the debate is still on as to whether he had a restrained or virulent type of the disease in his system. Schemann popularized Lagarde's anti-Semitic writings.

Wilhelm Richard Wagner fled to Switzerland as a revolutionary in 1848. He returned to Germany a convert to reaction. His disciples made Bayreuth, his burial place, holy ground. In the earlier period he wrote an outline of a drama centering in Jesus of Nazareth which was withheld from publication some four decades. Deserting Jesus for Buddha, Judaeo-Christian optimism for oriental pessimism, he sought to purify Christianity from Jewish fundamentals. Thus, because of frustration through the failure of the revolution, he developed from an advocate of the ethics of Jesus, of romantic liberalism, into an advocate of the Buddhist way of life. Instead of promoting the best interests of humanity he sought release in freedom from desire. Progress through revolution was a hopeless quest. Democracy was a phantom of editors. Gobineau's racialism solved his problem: Judaism was the victim. Hence he worked for a return to German mythology and deliverance from Jewish optimism. Only a Christianity separated from Jewish assumptions would do.

Adolf Stoecker, theologian, political journalist, member of the Prussian legislature and of the Reichstag, court preacher with the weekly circulation of his sermons 130,000, opponent of liberal theologians, directed his eloquence against Judaism.

Then there was Houston Stewart Chamberlain of English-German-Swedish descent, son-in-law of Wagner. Chamberlain's *Foundations of the Nineteenth Century*, published at the turn of the twentieth century, was the Blitz-attack upon Judaism. Within three years four editions proved necessary and a score before the attack had run its course. The Kaiser was so impressed by this "Bible of racialism" that he gave it his endorsement and it became a "decisive influence on a whole generation of young Germans and the inspiration of the entire Nazi literature." For seventy-five years German Protestantism dreamed about its glorious past, its grand future, its unshakable foundations, its mission to the world, and then listened to Karl Barth and his depreciation of man while *Volksreligion* was placing an atomic bomb at the foundations of Christianity.

Translations of *The Foundations of the Nineteenth Century* advertised anti-Semitism the world over. Built out of the racial views of Gobineau, Lagarde, and Wagner with several new suggestions, it traced the evolution of Europe from Greek art, Roman law, and the teachings of Jesus.

A few of its astounding errors are: Although born in Galilee Jesus was not a Jew but probably an "Aryan." Naturally he borrowed his emphasis upon the will from Judaism. The history of the West has been a conflict between "Aryans" and Semites. The Jew is a species of *homo Syriacus*. Race determines human development. The influence of the Semite upon the earlier kinds of Christianity destroyed the classical culture. But then the new Germanic blood which flowed into the arteries of the Graeco-Roman civilization revived it. Roman Catholicism attempted to block the Germanic revision of Christianity but in vain. Its fight in behalf of the intellectual, moral, and religious qualities of Judaism was lost.

Chamberlain's "Aryan" Jesus was no Buddha fleeing from the world. Jesus admired the beautiful, was at home in the world, and represented the dawn of a new day. "He won for the old human nature a new youth. Thus he became the God of the young, vigorous, Indo-European races, and under the sign of the cross there slowly arose upon the ruins of the old world a new culture"—which it became the mission of contemporary Germany to promote.

Nazism with all this "racial Christianity" at its disposal hurried the process of substituting Germanic religion for Christianity. *Mein Kampf* reverberates with paranoid shrieks against Judaism, the Bible, and Christianity. Hitler ranted and raved about an "Aryan" race when there was at most an "Aryan" language. The word "Aryan" dates from only 1794 when it was used to denote a people speaking one of the Indo-European languages. Max Mueller, who later denied there was an "Aryan" race, "Aryan" blood, "Aryan" eyes and hair, unfortunately in 1853 employed "Aryan" of race and gave the Germans this mischief-making start.

In Czarist Russia the spurious Protocols, deriving ultimately from a political satire published in 1864 and written in no relation to the Jews, was transformed into a polemic against the Jews. Discredited by historians and the courts of various countries, it was popularized in the United States, returning to Germany in this American modification to be exploited by Nazism.

There are many reasons for anti-Semitism. Religious prejudice cannot be ruled out. The general failure of Christians to believe in and practice the ethical standards of Christianity is another reason. The rise of pseudoscientific theories of race origin and what results from race mixture is a third reason. Business competition is also present. The gradual equalization of the rights of labor with those of capital is blamed by many upon the organizing genius and brains of the Jew. The Jews constitute a minority group in most countries. The Jewish cultural achievements are considerable. The Jew has an international outlook upon life.

After casting *Mein Kampf* aside as unworthy of serious attention regarding the roots of German anti-Semitism, one rereads it to discover just why Hitler hated the Jews. Dismissing the rhetorical embellishment one comes upon these underlying reasons for the Hitlerian propaganda. The Jews were to be cancelled out of the life of Germany because they helped the Allies win the war of 1914–1918; because they are internationally minded; because they believe in democracy; because they believe in representative government; because they proposed Esperanto as a common world language; because "Karl Marx was a Jew"; because Judaism claims to be a religion and not a race; because Judaism has the audacity to insist upon a destiny.

Now at last the menace in Hitlerian anti-Semitism has been clarified. It was directed not only against Judaism but also against the American way of life. Nazism and its antithesis, democracy, Hitler knew could not coexist in Germany. Neither could a genuine Christianity long approve of Nazism. But a frontal attack upon Christianity would be too heroic and too costly. It would be wiser to begin with eradication of the Jew and his Bible, the Old Testament of Christianity. Here a few Nazi paragraphs are pertinent:

> The Old Testament as a Book of Religion must be done away with, once and for all. In this way we shall bring to an end the vain effort of the last 1,500 years to transform us mentally into Jews—an effort to which we owe, among other things, our present material Jewish domination.

> This coming age will have a place for the Cathedral of Strassburg and the Wartburg, but it will repudiate the presumption of Rome as well as the Jerusalemitic Old Testament.

> It was the greatest sin of Protestantism that instead of paying attention to it [the gospel of German mysticism] it popularized the so-called Old Testament as a Book of the People [Volksbuch] and gave divine rank to the writings of the Jews.

With the Jew and his Bible destroyed, the purging and abolition of the New Testament would be in order and the racial chimera of that man Gobineau could become the basis of a racialized Reichskirche. Mein Kampf would be the authorized verbally inspired, errorless German Bible with no alterations of text permitted. Only Mein Kampf would lie on Nazi altars and to its left a sword. The father of a child would promise to rear it in the spirit of racialism having first affirmed its "Aryan" descent. The mother would repeat these vows. On the day of the founding of the National Church, "the Christian cross must be removed from all churches, cathedrals and chapels within the Reich and its colonies and must be replaced by the only unconquerable symbol, the Hakenkreuz, or swastika." In a word "the future Church of the Germans will be a united People's Reich-State Church on a Nordic religious basis or it will not exist."

Well, the millennial Nazi Reich ended after twelve years of horror, and anthropology long ago refuted the guesses of that man Gobineau on which Hitler's Reich was built. But why were the churches of Germany so feeble in their opposition to the "Nordic religious basis"? Was the underlying reason their refusal to abandon the medieval religious synthesis and construct a synthesis which twentieth-century western religion needs so desperately? The civilization of Europe has visibly broken with the medieval way of life, but religion has failed to keep pace with the change. Some wonder whether there would have been any Christian opposition to anti-Semitism in Germany if there had been no Jewish members of Christian churches.

Chapter Three

San Francisco and Greenland's Icy Mountains

Religions persist on the conviction that they are one and only. From the largest religious groupings numbering hundreds of millions of adherents to the tiniest sects below the one hundred mark, faith in their finality, in their uniqueness, compels them both to fight for survival and to conduct propaganda for converts. Although all religions are subject to the law of change, they must one and all claim to be today what they were thousands of years ago. All religions are "always, everywhere, the same." Acknowledgment of change spells disintegration. Science hails the discoveries of new truth. Religions deny it. Science is forward-looking. Religions look backward. For probably six decades Christianity looked forward, but it was then creedless, without a New Testament, without a hierarchy. From Clement I on, the reminiscent interpretation prevails, and creeds and apostolic succession and New Testament are built into the rising structure to make it a monument to the past. For eighteen centuries Christianity has been hostile to adjustments. They come but too slowly and too unintelligently. Moreover, this religious lag is taking a heavy toll in enthusiastic support of the Christian enterprise.

The San Francisco conference of the United Nations and the Charter it adopted have written finis over old-line, sectarian missionary effort. But within American Christian groups there is schism over the proper attitude toward missions. With a death struggle for survival ahead in the new Eastern world, American Christianity argues over verbal inspiration and virgin birth. Now the peoples invited to accept Christianity as superior to their native religions may care about other matters. A Chinese student, when asked what the most living religious question in China was, replied, "extraterritoriality." Even in defeat the Japanese observe the rules of their etiquette, not those of Emily Post. If long ago denominational boards had taken to heart the experience of Francis William Newman with the Mohammedans he attempted to convert, the Laymen's Missionary Inquiry would have been unnecessary. "While at Aleppo," Newman related, "I one day got into a religious discussion with a Mohammedan carpenter, which left on me a lasting impression. Among other matters I was peculiarly desirous of disabusing him of the current notion of his people, that our Gospels are spurious narratives, of late date. I found great difficulty of expression, but the man listened to me with much attention, and I was encouraged to exert myself. He waited patiently till I had done and then spoke to the following effect: 'I will tell you, sir, how the case stands. God has given you English a great many good gifts. You make fine ships and sharp pen-knives, and good cloth and cotton; you have rich nobles and brave soldiers; you write and print many learned books; all this is of God. But there is one thing that God has withheld from you and has revealed to us, and that is, the knowledge of the true religion, by which one may be saved.' When he had thus ignored my argument and delivered his simple protest, I was silenced and at the same time amused. But the more I thought it over the more instruction I saw in the case."

Returning from a visit to Australia, the New Hebrides, Japan, and China, in 1890, Henry Drummond addressed College Session in Edinburgh on missions, observing that there were two views of missions: "the world is lost and must be saved; the world is sunken and must be raised." To go abroad to rescue "heathen" is as absurd "as for a planter to go anywhere abroad in the hope of sowing general seed and producing general coffee." When the missionary "reaches his field, his duty is to find out what God has sown there already; for there is no field in the world where the Great Husbandman has not sown something. Instead of uprooting his Maker's work, and clearing the field of all plants that found no place in his small European herbarium, he will rather water the growths already there and continue the work at the point where the Spirit of God is already moving." Drummond pleaded for the type of missionary who was also "the Christian politician, the apostle of a new social order, the moulder and consolidator of the state. . . . He is not the herald but the prophet of the cross." "The christianizing of a nation like China or Japan is an intricate, ethical, philosophical and social as well as Christian problem." "It is the deliberate opinion of many men who know China intimately, *who are missionaries themselves*, that half of the preaching and especially the itinerating preaching, carried on throughout the empire, is absolutely useless. . . . In Tokio, I had the privilege of addressing some thirty or forty Japanese Christian pastors. At the close I asked them if they had any message they would like me to take home to the churches here or in America. They appointed a spokesman who stood up and told me in their name that there were two things they would like me to say. One was, 'Tell them to send us one six thousand dollar missionary rather than ten two thousand dollar missionaries.' The other request went deeper. I again give you the exact words, 'Tell them that we want them to send us no more doctrines. Japan wants Christ.'" A charge of heresy against Drummond rather than changes in missionary methods resulted.

Here is the philosopher Keyserling in Salt Lake City

being told by a girl who had come all the way from Munich in Germany because she believed in Mormonism: " 'God has proclaimed through Joseph Smith that he who petitions Him for knowledge in truthfulness will be answered directly, and He is as good as His word: that is how I was converted. I am a Munich girl; it was by accident that I listened to a Mormon missionary; he showed me how I could be certain of the divine origin of the Book of Mormon. So I asked God—and behold: He answered me at once with an audible Yes! Since then I am here and I am very happy.' . . . I looked at her and was really touched. . . . I had never heard with my own ears such touchingly simple ideas expressed." Perhaps we in our atomic age had best abandon hair-splitting theological arguments and resort to simple truths.

Gandhi, so often acclaimed a Christian, does not desire the conversion of India to Christianity. "If instead of confining themselves to humanitarian work such as education, medical services to the poor and the like, Christian missionaries would use these activities of theirs for the purpose of proselytizing I would certainly like them to withdraw. Every nation considers its own faiths to be as good as that of any other. Certainly the great faiths held by the peoples of India are adequate for her people. India stands in no need of conversion from one faith to another."

Marquis Ito's opinion of Christianity was not very flattering to it: "What is any religion, Buddhism or Christianity, but superstition and therefore a possible source of weakness to a nation? I do not regret the tendency toward free thought and atheism which is almost universal in Japan because I do not regard it as a source of danger to the community."

Commenting upon the Korean revolutionary movement, a Japanese newspaper editor wrote: "Christianity as taught by Protestant missionaries . . . puts a divine discontent into the heart of the oppressed. . . . The missionaries make bad hearts of the people and teach democracy."

A leader of the Chinese Student Movement also did not endorse Christian missions: "Christianity is a foreign religion; it persuades people to think more highly of foreign culture than of China's own; it propagates its own superstitions which are no less fantastic and harmful to all scientific understanding of the world than the grossest absurdities of Taoism and Buddhism. Its missionaries interpose themselves between worthless converts and the orderly processes of law. . . . Chinese Christians are the 'running dogs' of the imperialists."

A competent American authority on the Far East has written: "From the history of Christian missions of China, Japan, and Korea, one conclusion stands out sharply. Much harm and little good has come from governmental patronage and protection of missionary work and the missionary renders the most enduring service to the people among whom he labors, when he separates himself farthest from political concerns." In a popular philosophical treatise upon the religions of the world, the learned author severely criticizes the culture of the earlier missionaries: "I wish the missions would be forbidden on the part of governments. Their single members are often altogether venerable, but in moral culture they stand, almost without exception, too far below those whom they come to 'convert' not to do much more harm than good. One should not send hobbledehoys as teachers to cultured people, even if they are better men."

An American traveller in Ceylon quotes a native thus: "I am a Christian always when I am in school or talking to missionaries. . . . There is but one true religion: He who is seeking the true religion . . . will find it right here in our island of Ceylon. . . . Nearly all the people of Ceylon who would learn from the Christians, who are hungry and poor or who would have work, pretend the religion of the white man. For we receive more, the teachers are our better friends if we tell them we are Christians. . . ."

But the great surprise came during the war against Japan when a Japanese Christian published *Japan, the Land of the Gods and Christianity*. His Emperor is "manifest deity," but he believes also in God the Spirit, Creator and Preserver of Heaven and Earth, and feels no conflict or contradiction. For the Japanese "Emperor is directly descended from the ancestral Sun-Goddess, the Foundress of our country. . . . For the Christian, when he believes in the unseen God, the Lord of Heaven and Earth, in addition to the Emperor, does his feeling towards the Emperor change? No change ought to arise. It cannot arise, for His Imperial Majesty's direct descent from the Sun-Goddess is a strictly historical fact." Moreover, the Emperor is infallible: "We believe that the command of the Emperor is the command of God." The Bible is the Japanese Christian's guide to faith, but the Emperor's Rescript on Education is his guide to action! Japan is the "country of the gods founded by divine will. . . . We believe it unconditionally, uncritically, nay instinctively." "The Emperor is the State." "*In a word the Japanese State is the living model of the Kingdom of God.*" Shintoism came down out of heaven, and Christianity has the unique mission of giving moral inspiration to the Japanese, who alone are ruled according to the will of God. Christianity supplements Japanese mythology and nationalism.

But Christian churches in the United States, convinced that Christianity alone came down out of heaven whereas other religions are of this earth, assumed that the adherents of non-Christian religions stood with open arms to welcome the missionaries. On September 6, 1883, the *Independent* ran an editorial beginning: "It is not an extravagant anticipation that Japan may become a Christian nation in seventeen years. The Christian missionaries in Japan are now working with a strong hope that the twentieth century will open upon that island empire no longer a foreign missionary field but predominantly Christian, converted from the shadowy paganism and vague philosophies which now retain but a feeble hold upon the people and received into the brotherhood of Christendom. A Japanese Constantine is not far off." From Japan will "go forth a mighty influence to convert all Asia" to Christianity.

It is early 1946. The American Committee for the World Council of Churches just back from Japan reports Japan "wide open" to the Christian gospel—the old optimism returns! Apparently there is also some belated caution: "Indeed, there is some concern about the growing popularity of Christianity, lest it simply be a mass movement growing out of a sense of frustration as people have become aware of the bankruptcy of their old system." Why not add also accommodation to military coercion, fear, hope of reducing the period of military occupation and getting started once more on their own way of life? Beware of the identification of American Christianity with the policies of the military lest when the reaction comes Christianity be blamed for any of the military government's shortcomings!

In the closing years of the nineteenth century a prominent American missionary statesman reported that "in America, Europe, Australasia, and some of the great mission fields of Asia there is the impression that the work of missionaries in Japan is nearly if not entirely accomplished"! How the slogan "the evangelization of the world *in this generation*" then captured the imagination of the American student world! The enthusiastic faith of thousands of young men and women was re-enforced by Matthew 24:34, Mark 13:30, Luke 21:32, containing "*this generation*." Alas, it was forgotten that "*this generation*" ended about A.D. 70, that "all the world" was Palestine or at most the Mediterranean area, that Matthew 28:16–20, which orders the conversion of all nations, reflects merely a hope of the late first-century Christian community. Despite the words of the Biblical passage, we cannot accept it as a command of Jesus.

At the conference of the United Nations in San Francisco, May–June, 1945, the sessions were not opened with the speaking of Christian prayers. This vividly reminded Christians listening in that in the United States the active members of all the Christian churches constitute less than a third of the population and in the world no more than 27 per cent. Protestants may claim 6 per cent in that 27 per cent on rosy estimates. Mohammedanism is credited with 10.2 per cent and Judaism with less than .5 per cent. About 73 per cent of the world's religious population is non-Christian. The ratio in favor of magic and fetishism, worshippers of the state primitives, Hindus, Buddhists, Confucianists, Mohammedans, and so on is sixteen to one as far as Protestantism is concerned and five to one as far as the totality of Catholics is concerned. The fourteen missionaries per million people in China face a Herculean labor. Missions must be rethought in spite of missionary boards.

How did Christians think of their mission to the non-Christian world when the nineteenth-century missionary age dawned? The general objective was the conversion of the "heathen" into members of the particular Christian churches or sects under an assumed directive of the risen Jesus: "Go therefore and disciple all the nations, immersing them into the name of the Father and of the Son and of the Holy Spirit; teaching them to observe all things whatever I commanded you. . . ." Christians were God's children; non-Christians were "heathens." By hypothesis, these "heathens" were standing on Greenland, in India, in Africa, upon the islands of all the seas pleading with the Christians to deliver their lands from errors' chains. Missionary Boards selected missionaries on the basis of conformity to orthodox standards, told them what to preach and how to behave, paid their salaries, provided for the education of their children, granted them furloughs, and "housed them better than the average pastors of our churches at home." Agricultural missions were frowned upon; God did not send his apostles to teach the Burmese how to raise better cattle! Medical missionaries were not to concern themselves with operations and diets and health exercises but with the conversion of the sick to Christianity. You entered the hospital a "heathen," you departed a convert. Missionaries had not been sent to China to teach Western civilization but only so to direct education as to increase the adherents of their stations. The missionary was to save the souls of all the Negroes in Africa, of all the Chinese, Japanese, Koreans, Burmese, Indians from sin and Satan to Christianity in its hundred bewildering forms.

But the natives of the Far East looked upon the Christian missionaries as foreigners, and the governments remembered that consent to their presence was often forced upon them. The political issue could not be evaded. Missionaries were the beneficiaries of special national arrangements such as treaties, extraterritoriality, foreign concessions, toleration clauses. Could missionaries effectually proclaim themselves to be ambassadors of Christ when every "heathen" knew they were under the protection of their home governments which might intervene and even declare war in case of violation of the concessions? Would the government whose citizen the missionary was collect reparations for damage to mission property? Was the missionary an American, British, German nationalist, or a disciple of the Master? When the American missionary in India takes an oath pledging himself thereby "to undertake to do nothing contrary to or in diminution of the authority of the lawfully constituted government in the country to which he is appointed" and his Board has already pledged itself to "support the lawfully

constituted constitutional government, to abstain from political affairs, loyally cooperating with the government, to
employ only loyal missionaries and help missionaries to be
loyal," and when the native thereupon observes that government official and missionary profess the same religion
and attend the same church, will he not classify the American missionary as a nationalist rather than as a minister of
Christ?

The war of 1914 to 1918 fought largely by Christians
against Christians aroused the peoples of Africa and Asia
to reconsider the West and its religion. The native Christian
churches also began to rethink their relation to western
Boards. The Japanese Christian churches insisted upon
autonomy and an Oriental type of Christianity. The missionary was demoted from leader to consultant. The scandal
of Fundamentalism invaded the Far-East Christian
churches. Missionaries were recalled charged with being
"unsound" in the faith. Later Japanese Christians told Chinese Christians of their duty to kill them in case of war.
Christianity, said the Orient, perpetuates the white man's
domination. After the betrayal of Abyssinia, Christianity
suffered eclipse. And an American mission's stalwart reported that "there is a serious peril in more than one field
that these churches may become separated from historical
Christianity, creedal Christianity, ecumenical Christianity,
applied Christianity, vital Christianity." It was belatedly
admitted that two hundred and fifty million persons were
not within Christian range. The original slogan was revised
a little: ". . . the evangelization of the world in this generation did not mean the conversion of the world in a generation or its Christianization in a generation, nor was it a
prophecy of what was likely to take place; nor did its advocates ever stand for any hasty or superficial preaching of the
gospel or neglect of the resolute application of the gospel
to the obstinate social facts. It does mean that it is the duty

of each generation of Christians to bring the knowledge of Christ to its own generation."

In the presence of the new nationalisms in Asia, old-style missionary effort was proving inadequate. Successful missions required changes in method and the liberalization of Christian theology and the acceptance of the findings of the history of religions. The choice lay between discounting the uniqueness of Christianity and failure.

A group of Protestant denominations undertook the Laymen's Missions Inquiry. Seven volumes of genuine research material upon conditions in the Orient, "fact finders' reports" plus a digest and *Rethinking Missions*, resulted. Privately undertaken investigations also made their appearance. Today the true story of Eastern missions is available in hundreds of libraries the country over. Only a few of the alarming discoveries are mentioned here.

"It is exceedingly difficult to teach Japanese women about the Christian religion." In 1928 there were 27,210 paid women religious workers in Japan, only 248 of them Christian. The final results of settlement work were declared to be "not very significant." "There are missionaries at present in Japan who are widely respected and beloved. . . . There are, however, at the same time missionary workers who, although well intentioned, are lacking in qualities of personality and leadership. . . ." "The number of theological seminaries should be reduced from twelve to two or three." The curriculum must be made over along practical, social, humanitarian lines. "Mission Boards in America must arrange for churches in Japan to take the initiative in asking for missionaries." The Japanese rural church leaders were found to be superior to the Christian missionaries.

In China not more than one one-thousandth of the population was actively identified with Protestant Christianity. The decline in American missionaries, 1927 to 1931, came to 23 per cent. Between 1922 and 1934, the number of men of college grade in theological schools dropped 73 per cent and the graduates sought YMCA and YWCA positions, not pastorates. A late estimate of adherents of foreign religions in China gives Mohammedanism 48,104,241; Catholicism 3,262,678; Protestantism about half a million communicant members.

In Burma the verdict was "Both the missions and the churches have been primarily interested in the saving of souls. Practically nothing has been done to improve the physical and social conditions of the people. There are mission schools and hospitals but the underlying motive in maintaining them seems to be to secure a place for preaching."

Of India, Paton wrote: "At least 80 per cent of the Christians in India of the non-Roman communions have come directly or at one or two removes from the untouchable or depressed classes. . . . But in the East, Christianity is weak, relatively young, associated with foreign adventure or rule, and even today acknowledged by perhaps only 1 per cent of the masses of India." Reports "from Protestant schools show that the great majority of boys attending mission secondary schools and colleges are non-Christians and that few of these Hindu and Moslem boys are converted to Christianity while attending these institutions. . . ." The economic motive prevailed with many Indians who adopted Christianity.

Unusual publicity was given the Hocking report entitled *Rethinking Missions* in the daily press of the United States. One could not escape the discussion of missions in clubs, restaurants, and around the cracker barrel. It proposed the separation of educational and other philanthropic aspects of mission work from evangelism, co-operation with non-Christian agencies for social improvement, the understanding of native religions, the cessation of attacks upon non-Christian systems of religion, better missionaries with

nationals passing upon permanency, wider Christian fellowship for sympathizers with Christian principles unable to
affiliate with the churches, improvement of Christian educational institutions, personnel, and methods, the transfer
of responsibility to the native leaders, the unification of
American Boards. These too modest suggestions were
attacked by the Mission Boards of various denominations,
by Fundamentalism, by many missionaries.

Despite this official and orthodox reaction, a new interpretation of missions cannot be avoided. "The purpose of
foreign missions is not the establishment of an institution
or a church but the incubation of an ideal." The new
marching orders are ethical, not theological. When two
score candidates and one hundred and fifty-one missionaries answered a questionnaire on their reasons for desiring
to engage in mission effort 74 per cent old-line answered
affirmatively on divine call but only 40 per cent of the
candidates; 100 per cent of the former believed there was
greater need for religious experience over there but only
42.5 per cent of the latter; the old-line missionaries had not
expected to get anything but only to give, whereas 22.5 per
cent of the candidates hoped to get; and not one of the
candidates supported the earlier reasoning that the burden
of proof was upon anyone remaining in the homeland.
Only 2.5 per cent of the candidates entered the command
of Christ as a reason for being a missionary but 46.6 per
cent old-line missionaries did (as well as 40 per cent of the
ministers and 58.1 per cent of the laity involved in the
study).

Personal evangelism is surrendering to social Christianity.
Indigenous churches and native Christian leadership are in
the ascendancy. The intelligent missionary feels obliged to
promote Christian unity rather than denominational divisiveness, the ethics of Jesus in preference to dogma. He
understands that Christianity is not the one and only

religion, encourages the convert to live on in the old environment, and avoids competition for converts. He urges internationalism and world unity, not trade and nationalism. Consecration must be accompanied by a much higher ability and quality of preparation in the candidate for the foreign field today. "The human side of missions has been unduly weak." "Heathen" has become "non-Christian." "The Christian will regard himself as a co-worker with the forces within each religious system which are making for righteousness."

In the judgment of a Chinese scholar, "the future of Protestant missions in China from the Fundamentalist point of view is not bright, because Chinese scholars in general are not interested in theological problems and evangelism. China's interest in science will certainly grow with reconstruction. While China's rebirth needs religion, it will certainly not welcome those religious dogmas obviously contradictory to science. The future of Protestant missions from the *Rethinking Missions* point of view is fair. That from the humanist or ethical point of view is definitely bright. The Chinese are fundamentally humanists, and the most successful contributions Christianity has made to China have been along social and ethical lines."

In *The Evangelization of the World in This Generation* occurs the ominous statement: "Very many Christians entertain the belief that Christianity is not the absolute religion." Did "very many" become the great intelligent majority at San Francisco? If non-Christian nations can meet on the basis of perfect equality with the representatives of Christian nations in political forums and if world federation is on the way, can sectarian western cults any longer hope to conquer the ancient Oriental religions? The United Nations are "fighting for a better world, in terms of human values common to all religions," not "like the crusaders for a better Christian world." No one can state the new objective in religion better than Alfred Martin did when he proposed this creed:

I believe in a fellowship that shall unite men, not in bonds of Confucian, or Mohammedan, or Christian love, but in the holier bonds of human love; going down, beneath all that separates and estranges, to the principles of freedom and understanding; beneath religions to religion; beneath all the sacraments to the universal impulse that bends the soul in reverence and awe; beneath all forms to the faith that strives to express itself in and through them, thus touching common foundations and securing a common fellowship, each helping the other by whatsoever his deeper insight may reveal; a union, not of religious systems, but of free souls,—united, to build up, on the basis of truth, justice, and love, the divine Commonwealth of Man.

In the American Protestant-Jewish-Catholic formulation of ten goals for the San Francisco meeting much is made of international law, justice, good of the world community, economic rights, political and economic well-being, cultural development and political responsibility with only this reference to religion in number nine: "The Charter should include an international bill of rights and provide for a commission or commissions to protect and further the rights and liberties of the individual and of racial, religious, and cultural groups especially those uprooted by war or oppression."

And the Charter of the United Nations opposes any distinctions "as to race, sex, language, or religion." Its objectives are "economic, social, cultural, and humanitarian." The fundamental human freedoms are to be respected, and against woman there is to be no discrimination. Christianity in the one world of the future is e pluribus unum.

Chapter Four

The American Social Gospel *

There has been a socially minded Christianity from Jesus of Nazareth to *Quadragesimo Anno*. Monotheism demands internationalism. In the Old Testament stern criticisms of the oppression of the poor, economic injustice and extortion, corruption in high places, slavery, infringement upon human rights abound. The gospel of Jesus includes a comprehensive ethical and community emphasis—the eschatological framework to the contrary notwithstanding. The Kingdom of God for the early Christian "lay principally in the domain of the future and wholly in the domain of the miraculous," but he loved his neighbor in very practical ways. To Constantine, almsgiving and works of mercy, the care of those imprisoned in the mines, and the support of needy churches enlisted his sympathy and aid. In the later medieval age "production was subordinated to consumption," money-making was restricted by social need, a "just

* In many articles and reviews, the author has more fully interpreted the history of the Social Gospel. Some of these are: *Crozer Quarterly*, Oct. 1944, review of the Umphrey Lee, *Historic Church and Modern Pacifism*; *ibid.*, Jan. 1946, "Walter Rauschenbusch and his Interpreters"; "Introduction" to Frick's German translation of *The Prayers for the Social Awakening*; "Social Gospel," in *An Encyclopedia of Religion*, 1945; *Review of Religion*, 1941, review of Hopkins, *Rise of Social Gospel in American Protestantism*, easily the best book in the field; *Rochester Theological Seminary Bulletin, Rauschenbusch Number*, Nov., 1918, a comprehensive discussion of his life and books and the basis of much that appears in subsequent interpretations; *The Colgate-Rochester Divinity School Bulletin*, vol. I, no. 1, vol. IV, no. 4, and vol. VI, no. 4.

price" theory prevailed, the holding of private property was defended as incentive to work, and emphasis was laid on social co-operation and peace, almsgiving, and exhortation to temperance.

Christianity lost control of wealth in the seventeenth century and acquiesced in the taking of interest because of the chaos created by the wars of religion, the rapid expansion of business and trade, the inability of Protestant churches to enforce discipline, the accumulation of wealth through thrift, the rise of an individualism which would not trust any man, the beginning of the money-market. Salmasius formulated the new argument in behalf of Christian interest. It ran like this: The banker is a necessity, not a luxury. The abolition of banking would merely make the borrower the prey of worse usurers. The prosperous big business man could not make use of the business opportunities before him without access to capital which only the Lombardian bankers could supply. *The business man paid a high rate of interest, but the available capital made it possible for him to purchase in quantity at a much lower price. And the interest went into cost.* The French peasants were living in dire poverty because the Lombardians were not operating in France.

Moreover, the taking of interest was in accordance with and not opposed to natural law. Money is not merely exchange as Aristotle had taught but the equivalent of barter, ware, goods. The money-lender is a public benefactor even when he charges interest. Salmasius asked precisely how rent from money, that is, interest, differed from rent for a house or a field. *Interest ethically is the gratitude experienced by the borrower toward his benefactor!* Again, unless the borrower pays interest, the situation of equality existing before the loan was made is not restored. The advantage the borrower obtained by receiving the loan must be equalized through the payment of interest.

Interest is both economically necessary and ethically sound. But is interest Christian? Salmasius answered, yes. For Christ nowhere forbade interest. The Sermon on the Mount directs that in lending, a man's ability to repay should not form the basis of the loan. Should a Christian lend, not expecting the return of the loan? That would be ideal. *Yet not every Christian can realize the ideal. There are perfect and imperfect Christians. The gospel contains commands and also counsels.* Imperfect Christians are nevertheless useful Christians. The average man can only be expected to live within the law. *Interest-giving is right. A Christian voluntarily gives interest.* Therefore, he certainly can raise no objection to the taking of interest. But to make the taking of interest a business, to turn capitalist, would be unethical.

Calvinism continued to seek the Christianization of the social order. In Massachusetts, for example, American Puritans proceeded on the assumption of a divine mandate. They meant to labor for the glory of God and the advancement of the Christian faith. God, absolute and arbitrary, had selected a few of their company for heaven. There were two covenants, not only the covenant of grace but also that of works, namely, obedience to the code of ethical, social, and political ideas which Puritan researchers had discovered in the Bible, particularly in the Old Testament. This code the Puritan ministers sought to enforce in a visible Christian social order which, call it "bibliocracy" or "theocracy," was the seventeenth-century facsimile of the commonwealth of Israel. It was built around solidarity, collectivism, discipline, with sin a crime and church and state united. It was colonial Protestant social Christianity at its best. It disintegrated because free contract is antithetical to theocracy, local congregation to universal church, freehold tenure to year of jubilee, and property qualification for suffrage to church membership requirement for suffrage.

Another illustration of social Christianity is religious communism, which, based upon quotations from Jesus and upon the Jerusalem experiment described in Acts 2 and 4, found a great variety of expression in American cults. There were the Shakers, with inventions of Babbitt metal, brooms, cut nails, circular saws, Shaker flannel, clothespins, and so on to their credit, and with celibacy, pacifism, woman's rights, duality in deity in their creed. There were also Rappites, Battle Axes, Separatists of Zoar, New Harmony, Perfectionists of Oneida, Amana, Hutterian Brethren, and all the rest.

European and British and American Christian social Christianity exists in Catholic and Protestant types whose story would require a volume. Maurice von Ketteler, Leo XIII, Heath in Europe, and Channing, Bushnell, Theodore Parker, and a host of others here both recognized the social implications of the Gospel and fought for their practical application to the contemporary situation.

The American social gospel movement was essentially different from all this social expression of the Christian faith. That movement sought to harmonize the supernaturalism of Christianity's beginnings with the scientific and socio-economic patterns of the late nineteenth century. For the proletariat it was too ethereal; for the orthodox, too earthly. It did not regenerate economic determinism, and the churches still resist its infiltration.

To become more specific, for Fundamentalism it was "a college professor's new book" opposed on every page to "the old Book." Jesus saw corruption in government but commanded the people to pay taxes. He did not rebuke soldiers or condemn war. He announced that the age would end in violence. "He saw the saloon, the wine shop, and the drunkard at every corner; he organized no campaign against them and was never crowned and hailed as a prohibitionist." Poverty was to continue until his return. His healing of the sick and expulsion of demons were not for our imitation. His work was "Messianic," not socialistic. For over four decades American Fundamentalism has thus been sneering at the American social gospel.

Other criticisms of the American social gospel held up to scorn its claim of omniscience and its merely theoretical possibilities. It knew not how to prescribe remedies that would cure the ailing social order. It was an American discovery ignoring all the social action of the church through the centuries, unfamiliar with the medieval synthesis or the Geneva of Calvinism and the Massachusetts of the Puritans. It eliminated the supernatural from traditional Christianity and degraded other-worldly into next-worldly. It threw out the eschatological, mystical, sacramental aspects of Christian history. It was "Anglo-Saxon activism." Courses in Troeltsch, Weber, and Tawney were prescribed for this cultural astigmatism.

The American social gospel naively attempted to Christianize Marxism. It accepted "formed socialism" and assimilated it to the supernatural gospel instead of deriving its program from that gospel and sitting in judgment upon economic determinism. It was a "new Puritanism" sowing seeds of intolerance, exclusiveness, and the Eighteenth Amendment, alienating churchmen and youth from Christianity. Why did the social gospelers try to compromise with the traditionalists instead of boldly asserting that their gospel was different from the "Kingdom view" of the first Christians?

The modern business world attacked the social gospel as Utopian and occasionally published clipping-research against it. The two compilations of Henry B. Joy of Detroit, 1936, contain over 200 pages of sour quotes against the social gospel. American industrialists had made up their minds.

The major objective of the social gospel was to retain the

social values of the gospel in the modern world; its chief error was the abortive reconstruction of history in the interest of this good intention. The facts of history will not yield to allegorization or symbolism or "spiritual kinship" ideas. To fasten a twentieth-century process view of life, namely, organic development, upon a peasant of ancient Galilee is like expecting him to get rid of mosquitoes by spraying DDT by airplane over his swamps. The social gospel could not be born until economic determinism and Darwin's *Origin of Species* had appeared, and little is gained and much lost from ignoring this.

An American New Testament scholar has recently and with great clarity again emphasized what the Bible means by Kingdom of God: "However, nowhere in the New Testament or in the Biblical literature generally is the Kingdom of God viewed as a humanly-achieved new order of society. The roots of the conception are Semitic, not Greek; religious, not humanitarian or secular. From first to last the Biblical idea emphasizes the fact that it is *God's* reign. The emphasis is upon the character of the *King*, not upon the extent or nature or even duration of the realm he controls, though these are assumed to be final and absolute." *

Two associates of Walter Rauschenbusch in the social gospel movement came to see that modern reconstructions of ancient facts to achieve worthy goals cannot be justified. Shailer Mathew's *The Social Teaching of Jesus* was rewritten and revised into greater agreement with the eschatological emphasis in the early church. George D. Herron at first advocated the social gospel interpretation but later became just as certain that the transformation of Jesus into a later nineteenth-century economist could not be defended: "Jesus' view of life is inadequate to the social revolution" of the twentieth century. It is now too late for the social gospel to recant and start anew on a historical foundation.

* F. C. Grant, *An Encyclopedia of Religion*, p. 419.

But the method of procedure might originally have been otherwise, avoiding the futile discussion over the Kingdom of God. Consider the method followed by Congregationalism in 1925 when it formulated its statement of social ideals. The preamble of its declaration offered no argument regarding the modernization of the Kingdom of God concept. It employed as point of departure the combination quotation from Deuteronomy and Leviticus used by Jesus: Love of God and love of neighbor: "We believe in making the social and spiritual ideals of Jesus our test for community as well as for individual life; in strengthening and deepening the inner personal relationship of the individual with God, and recognizing his obligation and duty to society. This is crystallized in the two commandments of Jesus: 'Love thy God and love thy neighbor.' We believe this pattern ideal, for a Christian social order involves the recognition of the sacredness of life, the supreme worth of each single personality, and our common membership in one another—the brotherhood of all. In short, it means creative activity in co-operation with our fellow human beings, and with God, in the everyday life of society and in the development of a new and better world social order." Then the declaration translates these ancient ideals into modern applications in the areas of education, industry and economic relations, agriculture, racial relations, and international relations. This is historically sound, scientific, ethical, and practical. What Jesus would preach to this generation no one can say. That does not prevent religiously and ethically minded men of today from engaging in the reconstruction of the social order on their own. Why should they try to make themselves believe that what they think and do, that their transitory program, was in the mind of a religious teacher of the long ago? Why not select and adopt ancient ideals to the circumstances and needs of a new society?

The social gospel apparently fulfilled its mission by summoning young men and women to enthusiastic activity in the task of social reconstruction. It did not win labor to increased membership in the churches. It made individual ministers socially minded but did not alter the general direction of the American churches. It was an inspirational tonic, not a major operation upon the structure of society. It employed an authoritarian course of action to achieve democratic ideals. It appeared to endorse historical interpretation of the gospel and desired to save it for the modern world, but it effaced history in the effort. It fashioned a new synthesis in the attempt to compromise with the spirit of the times but insisted upon its ancientness. It paid the penalty anachronism imposes. It was new but refused to acknowledge its youth.

The ethical emphases of the Hebrew prophets, of Jesus, and of Christianity are in the stream of American life, but the great majority of American church members await the return of the departed Lord on the clouds of the sky to establish the millennium, or at least accept "the justificational view of human life." The regeneration of the individual is "the presupposition of a new social order." The Word must be preached. The world cannot be made over. Hitler and Mussolini and Japanese "co-prosperity" were authorized by God! The prophecy of the invention of the atomic bomb is in the Bible! Back to speaking in tongues, not forward to world brotherhood! Let the world become complete confusion and chaos that the Lord may return to judgment! The socially minded minorities in the various churches must learn how to co-operate with the great majority of Americans (who remain outside the churches) to secure the objectives of the American social gospel, which has run its course. Even social Christianity is now meeting bitter criticism within the churches. *Evidently, the reconstruction of the social order has become humanity's imperative task.* Those within the churches must work together with those outside, to attain common social ideals. *Had the social gospelers boldly declared this fifty years ago instead of making the futile and fatal appeal to a "given" first century, the agony of the transition to a one-world view, program, and organization might have been considerably reduced.*

Chapter Five

Religious Education

Christianity has a Janus-record in education. It has quoted Matthew 28:20 and I Corinthians 14:26 as educational marching orders and Acts 7:22 to approve the study of the Greek and Roman classics. It has also employed Matthew 11:25, 19:14 and Mark 10:15 in behalf of ignorance.* The *Didascalia* advises Christians to "keep away from the books of the heathen. What hast thou to do with the strange words, the laws, and the lying prophecies which tempt young people'from the faith? What fault hast thou to find with the word of God that thou stayest thyself upon heathen fables? Wilt thou read history? Thou hast the Book of Kings. Wise men and philosophers? Then thou hast the Prophets, in whom thou wilt find more wisdom and knowledge than in the wise men and philosophers, because theirs are the words of God, who alone is wise. Dost thou wish songs? Then thou hast the Psalms of David. An explanation of the world? Then thou hast Genesis by the great Moses. Laws and commandments? Thou hast the divine law in Exodus. Keep entirely away from all strange things which are in opposition to these."

This is an account of how Saint Jerome was punished for

* "Go into all the world . . . teaching;" "Moses was educated in all the learning of the Egyptians" on the one hand and ". . . things hidden from the wise [but] revealed unto babes" on the other.

reading Cicero: "And so, miserable man that I was, I would fast only that I might afterwards read Cicero. After many nights spent in vigil, after floods of tears called from my inmost heart, after the recollection of my past sins, I would once more take up Plautus. And when at times I returned to my right mind, and began to read the prophets, their style seemed rude and repellent. . . . Suddenly I was caught up in the spirit and dragged before the judgment seat of the Judge; and here the light was so bright, and those who stood around were so radiant, that I cast myself upon the ground and did not dare to look up. Asked who and what I was I replied: 'I am a Christian.' But He who presided said: 'Thou liest, thou art a follower of Cicero and not of Christ!'" There follows a description of the torture applied in punishment.

What Christians did to Hypatia does not make pleasant reading today. Waylaying the Alexandrian philosopher on her way home and "dragging her from her carriage, they took her to the church, called Caesareum. There they completely stripped her and murdered her with tiles. When they had torn her to pieces, they took her mangled limbs to a place called Cinaron and there they burnt them."

Appealing to God for assistance in his noble antagonism to education, Sir William Berkeley, governor of Virginia, wrote: "I thank God there are no schools nor printing, and I hope we shall not have them these hundred years; for learning has brought disobedience and heresy and sects into the world, and printing has divulged them, and libels against the best government. God keep us from both."

In the sixteenth century Cardinal Borromeo organized a Sunday School in Milan. As early as 1674, Roxbury, Massachusetts, had one. The Mennonites of colonial Pennsylvania were not unfamiliar with the institution. Robert Raikes began his humanitarian adventure in behalf of the neglected children of England toward the end of the eighteenth century. He desired to keep the "ragged, rough little factory children off the streets, to teach them how to read and write, to develop their personality and impart the word of God." In 1785, William Elliott, a Methodist layman, introduced the Sunday School into Virginia, whence it spread to the other states of the new nation, becoming the particular protegé of Protestantism.

Religious training in England's schools a century ago apparently matched the American Sunday School variety, if we may rely upon these questions and answers:

"Who gave you the name which you received at baptism?"
    "God."
"What did your god-father and god-mother promise and vow for you respecting the pomps and vanities of the world?"
    "All the sinful lusts of the flesh."
"Who were the Gentiles?"
    "A people of God."
"Who was Moses?"
    "An apostle of Christ."
"Who was Peter?"
    "An angel."
"Where was Christ crucified?"
    "In England."
"Who was Jesus Christ?"
    "A son of David."
"Who then was David?"
    "A son of Jesus."

One investigator concluded that the tests indicated a "vagrant state of mind, approaching to idiocy."

It was little improved in the early twentieth century, to judge from *The Army and Religion*, a report on religion in the British army during the war of 1914 to 1918: "That

probably four-fifths of the young manhood of our country
should have little or no vital connection with any of the
churches, and that behind this detachment there should lie
so deep a misunderstanding of the faiths by which Christian
men and women live, and the ideals of life which they hold,
is, perhaps, the most salient feature of the evidence. Here
is an alarming fact which is, surely, clear proof that something somewhere has gone gravely wrong, and that the hour
has come when we must discover the hidden causes of the
evil and do what may be done to set things right."

If one had attended every session of an American Sunday
School 1872 to 1917, he would have skipped 64.9 per cent
of the entire Bible and retained only faint memories of the
remaining 35.1 per cent. Nine books of the Bible were altogether omitted from the curriculum, but Daniel and Revelation were powerfully brought to the attention of the
scholars.

Until the war of 1914 to 1918, the American Sunday
School was meeting with some success. It never covered
much of the Bible in its weekly lessons. In its attitude toward the Bible it was lagging far behind the latest conclusions of science and historical method. But it was a
centre of inspiration and cohesion. Its equipment and ad-
ministration and teachers represented at least the median
of the group. Its leadership, instead of correctly diagnosing
the retardation then setting in, instead of redoubling its
efforts to increase interest and spending money, more and
more money, upon well-trained teachers, yielded to the
softly blowing south wind of good roads, a ride in the
model-T, meeting the God of nature and the hot dog supper out in the beautiful woods. Hence the church year
began with Thanksgiving Day and continued to Easter with
time off for Christmas and New Year. The concentration
upon Lent was followed by the march to the golf links in
April. Resuscitation of Sunday School attendance by way

of the "three period" plan has now issued in the last gasp of the Sunday School known as the "elective course."

The retardation in Sunday School enrollment in the United States as far as Protestantism is concerned came to over 30 per cent between 1916 and 1926. The actual decrease during the next decade amounted to much more.

Long before this, toward the end of the nineteenth century, the deficiencies of the Protestant Sunday School were evident to all leaders in education. A genuine attempt was therefore made by liberal leaders of American Protestantism to bridge the gap between the efficiency of public education and the antediluvian content of the Sunday School lessons. By revision of textbooks, training of teachers, grading, a very feeble use of historical method applied to the Bible, enthusiasts hoped to bring the Sunday School into step with its environment. But the great majority of Protestant Sunday Schools continued the use of older methods and materials and "paid" teachers were out. The dean of a midwest divinity school discussing the shortcomings of American education wittily described "high-brow" religious education thus: "A third specific guaranteed to cure is *Religious Education* with a capital R and a capital E. When I was graduated from a Methodist seminary sixteen years ago, religious education was a siren that lured some of my classmates from the 'traditional' pastorate to 'a more significant vocation.' 'R.E.,' as we affectionately called her, was the minister's ideal helpmeet and would make the education of the American people religious. But that was sixteen years ago, and the old lady is no longer the glamour girl she once was. Most of her ministerial boy friends are a *little self-conscious about their former intimacy*."

Durant Drake, observing the drift away from formal Christianity and its inability to assimilate millions of immigrants in American metropolitan areas, maintained that no more than one-half of the persons connected with the churches were interested and active. Reasons assigned included the rise in the cultural level, the failure of the home and of religious education. The religious educational system was failing because its leaders did not know what education and religion were and were attempting to train "the will to keep a code." Religious education had abandoned the catechism but had substituted only a slightly less antiquated view of the Bible for what had been. Contemporary problems were too dangerous for discussion in the graded lessons.

Others insisted that religious education was resulting in confusionism for modern youth which was seeking the abundant life apart from religion. The Hartshorne-May study concluded that the logical place to raise standards of moral knowledge of children was the home, that Sunday School teachers were neither directly nor indirectly contributing to moral knowledge, that "the child is influenced more by the group code than by an individual code, that the ratio between ethical standards of parents and children came to .545, that of Sunday School teachers and children to .002."

Professor G. H. Betts summarized the Hartshorne-May investigation thus: "From extensive tests given many children in such traits as cheating and copying in school work, telling lies about their own achievements, taking unfair advantages of others, etc., no relation was found between such conduct and the numbers of Sunday School attendants. Non-attendants made as good a record as regular attendants.

"Character traits investigated by the same men among other groups of children were: kindness and helpfulness, loyalty to their group, generosity, self-control. Here again no relation to Sunday School attendance was found, or so slight a relation as to be negligible.

"The correlation of moral knowledge (knowledge of

be punished much more in Hell. So God in his mercy called it out of the world in its early childhood.

Growing angrier than ever at Jesus, the high priest pressed him with further questions: "Tell us, are you the Christ, the Son of God?"
And Jesus answered: "That is what you have said."
That made the high priest furious. He stalked up and down and tore his clothes and beat the air with his hands. . . .
Great numbers of people made up the procession to Calvary, as Golgotha is known—heartless, cruel, blood-thirsty murderers. . . .

One wonders to what lengths an enthusiastic and dramatic teacher might go in commenting orally upon such suggestive sentences!
The critics of religious education have been clamoring for its revision along sociological lines. *The Encyclopedia of the Social Sciences* seems to endorse this demand. One turns to the topic "Religious Education" only to find: "See education, section on sectarian education." There thirty-five pages are devoted to education and four pages to sectarian education. Also the Sunday School is dismissed with "since the sixteenth century Sunday Schools have taught illiterate Europe and England to read the Bible." The instruction in the Sunday Schools has not dealt with the social-economic problems of modern life in any serious way.
The Protestant promoters of a higher type of religious education went down to defeat by the traditional Sunday School which obstinately resisted all their redemptive pressure. Trouble-making orthodox and fundamentalist ministers effectively blocked the introduction of the revised religious curriculum into the Sunday Schools. Sectarian teaching continued in the great majority of the Sunday

Schools, "antiquated, inadequate, inefficient, extravagant.
. . . No really successful system of religious education can
ever be built on the Sunday School method with its individual church and denominational approach." The traditional Sunday School won out over heretical religious
education. Yet, to survive, religious education must continue its protest. For religious instruction based upon the
historical study of the Bible contradicts teaching based
upon the ecumenical creeds and the confessions of faith
composed between 1530 and 1647, from the Augsburg Confession to that of Westminster. But religious education has
not and indeed cannot provide the religious synthesis humanity today longs for.

What has our study shown thus far? Authoritarianism
is helpless before the complicated religious issues of today.
Its partnership with the civilization of Europe is dissolving.
Meanwhile, racialism holds sway, Christianity's claim to
uniqueness has been surrendered, Christianity does not dare
to become too socially minded, and its educational system
needs a primary repair job.

Before examining the new synthesis which science and
history are offering the stricken world, we pause for a brief
summary of what has occurred during the past three centuries in the American environment.

Part Two

The American Scene

Chapter Six

From Harvard to the University of Alaska *

The story of the American university begins with the founding of Harvard by American Puritans in 1636. Its purpose is eloquently described in *New England's First Fruits:* "After God had carried us safe to New England and we had builded our houses, provided necessaries for our livelihood, reared convenient places for God's worship and settled civil government: One of the next things we longed and looked after was to advance learning and perpetuate it to posterity; dreading to leave an illiterate ministry to the churches, when our present ministers shall lie in the dust." The seal of Harvard expresses the original intention in *Christo et ecclesiae.*

In 1641 the management of Harvard was in charge of twelve overseers chosen by the general court, six of them magistrates and *six, ministers.* Latin and Greek were required for entrance. Every student was "earnestly pressed to consider well the main end of his life and studies to be, *to know God and Jesus Christ which is eternal life.*" The Scriptures were to be read twice a day. All profanation of God's name, attributes, word, ordinances, times of worship was to be "eschewed."

* The concise treatment of matters in Chapters Six to Nine, necessitated by limitations upon space, is expiated by fuller treatment of related matters in Chapters Five to Nine in the author's *School and Church: The American Way* (New York: Harper and Brothers, 1944). A paper edition may be had at $1 each, if purchased in quantity.

The charter of Harvard College bearing the date of 1650 defines the purpose of the institution to be the "education of the English and Indian youth of the country in knowledge and Godliness."

The minutes of the trustees of Yale, November 11, 1701, emphasize the interest of "our present religious govt." in the undertaking and the religious elements in the curriculum. The rector was to take especial care that the "said students be weekly (in such seasons as he shall see cause to appoint) caused memoriter to recite the assembly's Catechism in Latin and Ames's Theological Theses as also Ames's cases." The Scriptures were to be read twice daily. On the Sabbath the students non-graduated were to repeat sermons.

The Preamble to the Connecticut Act of 1742 makes it quite clear that "colleges are societies of Ministers for training up Persons for the work of the Ministry," for it states: "Whereas, by sundry acts and laws of this assembly, they have founded, erected, endowed, and provided for the maintenance of a college at New Haven which has (by the blessing of God) been very serviceable to promote useful learning and Christian knowledge, and, more especially to train up a learned and orthodox ministry for the supply of the churches. . . ."

About mid-eighteenth century a broadening of the base of the developing American university is discernible in the establishment of the University of Pennsylvania, although "theology" still heads the seven branches of knowledge. King's College, now Columbia, adds the advancement of the public good to the objective of the glory of Almighty God. On its library I Peter 2:1, 2, 7 reminiscently appears. But as to religion it is understood that "there is no intention to impress on the scholars the peculiar tenets of any particular sect of Christians." Four different denominations were represented among the trustees of Brown and it was "open to all denominations of Protestants" including Jews, according to President Manning. "Sectarian differences of opinions" were not to "make any part of the public and classical instruction" and no religious tests were ever to be admitted "into this liberal and catholic institution . . . but on the contrary all the members hereof shall forever enjoy full, free, absolute and uninterrupted liberty of conscience." In 1785, at the University of Georgia "all officers appointed to the instruction and government of the University" were to "be of the Christian religion."

Lest anyone conclude that college students in the good old times were superior to those of today consider this comparison:

> Statistics from 80 state institutions in 1921 show that out of a total enrolment of 152,461 students, 130,486 had religious affiliations, while 21,975 made no statement regarding their religious life. This is very encouraging when compared with our early history, when even though the colleges were church institutions, practically all the students were outside the church. In Princeton from 1778 to 1782 there was but one professor of religion. At Bowdoin College in 1807 there was only one Christian. At Yale for four years there was but one, and but four or five in other years about the beginning of the century. Many of the students assumed the name of leading infidels and atheists. Often every student was a professed infidel, or at least outside the church. Bishop Meade of Virginia said in 1811 that William and Mary College was a hotbed of French infidelity, and that for many years in every educated man he expected to find an infidel.

The revolutionary educational ideals of Thomas Jefferson suggested the pattern for the American university. During the Revolutionary War the school of sacred theology at

William and Mary was abolished. In 1787 Jefferson advised his nephew to study religion free from prejudice. After 1814 he always omitted theology from the subjects to be taught at the University of Virginia. His first list of books for the University included only about 10 per cent of religious and ecclesiastical history titles. In selecting professors he ignored their religious affiliations and refused to inquire into their religious attitude. Good humor, integrity, industry, and scientific knowledge were requirements for appointment. The professor of ethics was to deal with religious problems. Jefferson's general point of view is indicated in the following passage:

A professorship in Theology should have no place in our institution. . . . In our university you know there is no Professorship of Divinity. . . . A handle has been made of this to disseminate an idea that this is an institution not merely of no religion, but against all religion. . . . In our annual report to the legislature, after stating the constitutional reasons against a public establishment of any religious instruction, we suggest the expediency of encouraging the different religious sects to establish, each for itself, a professorship of its own tenets, on the confines of the University, so near as that its students may attend lectures there, and have the free use of the library, and every other accommodation we can give them: *preserving, however, their independence of us* and each other. This fills a chasm objected to in ours as a defect in an institution professing to give instruction in all useful sciences. I think the invitation will be accepted by some sects from candid intentions, and by others out of jealousy and rivalship. And by bringing the sects together, we shall soften their asperities, liberalize and neutralize their prejudices, and make the general religion a religion of peace, reason and morality.

What Jefferson was aiming at was an historical and scientific approach to the study of religion. Its true story was to be told. The student would hear about the origins of religion, its controversy with science, magic, ancestor worship, the mother goddess, the Easter bunny, child sacrifice, salmon rites, the Golden Rule of Confucius, relics, divinity of kings, charms, mana, the crux ansata, as well as about the story of the Bible.

In 1817 at Detroit a Protestant minister and a Catholic priest proposed the establishment of the Catholepistemiad or University of Michigan with the salary of the instructor or instructrix twice that of the professor. There were to be thirteen didaxiae or professorships ranging from universal science, literature, and mathematics to ethical sciences, military sciences, historical sciences, and, finally, intellectual sciences. The thirteenth didaxia was subdivided into the minds of animals, the human mind, spiritual existence, the Deity, and religion with the Vice President in charge of the instruction. Compare religion in the sixty-fourth place in this arrangement with *theologia* in first place in the University of Pennsylvania enumeration of colonial days, and the future of the American university may be foretold. Christianity has lost its uniqueness, since it is subsumed under intellectual science and religion. Later, at Ann Arbor, President Tappan, who had been a minister of the Dutch Reformed Church and deeply appreciated the American plan of the separation of church and state, concluded that an American state university could never tolerate a department of theology and therefore proceeded along the lines suggested by Jefferson.

This non-sectarian type of American university in the course of a century spread throughout the United States. In 1917, a hundred years after the founding of the University of Michigan, the University of Alaska was established, and the victory was complete. Freedom in investigation is taken for granted. The teacher is free to expound his own subject and does not pose as an authority in "controversial topics beyond his own field of study." Outside of college he has "precisely the same freedom and the same responsibility as attach to all other persons." The university exists not only to continue existing knowledge but also to stimulate research and the proper interpretation of new knowledge.

The American colonial colleges had precise religious objectives. Formal courses in religion were prescribed. The principle of separation of church and state imbedded in the constitution of the United States arrested sectarianism in education and condemned theological seminaries to cultural isolation. Thereupon, historical method was applied to the Bible and religion's past, science rapidly won the hegemony, the cultural level of America rose through public education. *The study of religion, therefore, became an educational subject.* At last the "comprehensive facts of religion as it has manifested itself throughout the ages" could be studied honestly, critically, sympathetically, without a sense of shame, in the college classroom. The "inspirational centre" emphasis vanished before the scientific, objective, historical approach to religion.

Several significant consequences are observable.

On the one hand, formal religion courses in various colleges and universities are discounted if not held in contempt. There are various reasons for this attitude. Courses in religion are taken because prescribed, because the coaches recommend them to athletes, because they are easy, and also as "extras." If the instructor employs historical method in courses upon the Bible, "pious" students are "upset," "bewildered," made "dizzy," and parents regard them as destructive of the "solid faith" with which Dot left home. If the instructor *mirabile dictu* uses "Bible School methods" the students object to the "Sunday School stuff." The instructor in either case starts with two strikes against him.

He "must" uphold traditional Christianity or the "religious" get busy. Moreover, he can do little for morale. For his remarks are discounted as prejudiced in favor of religion from the beginning. Else why is he making his bread and butter teaching it? One word in behalf of religion in a mathematics, sociology, or science classroom is worth a year's "preaching" in a religion class.

On the other hand, whereas formerly there was slight interest in religion in the university curricula because of the naive and dogmatic approach to its values, now in almost every course reference is made to religion because of its association with the advance or retardation of civilization, thought, society, government, education, music, art, and so on. Two decades ago a prominent American state university discovered that over four score courses in its catalogue had to concern themselves with religion. In courses in fine arts, anthropology, archaeology, biological and other sciences, the various languages ancient and modern, education, English, government, history, mathematics, music, philosophy, psychology, sociology, and so on, religious reference is unavoidable.

Religious people lament that religion is not taught in the American colleges and universities. The answer is that there is more religious instruction now than in the colonial colleges. But it is hidden, it is indirect, it is objective, it is educational. To clarify the situation, to protect itself against ignorant criticism, the university should boldly state its case. How? First, let it devote a couple of pages in its catalogue to advertise what it is really doing in religion. *Second, let it classify its courses in religion under science, education, English, history, music, philosophy and ethics, psychology, sociology where they now belong.* Students would then take religion courses seriously and be amazed to discover that their religious counselors were not telling them the truth when they warned them that religion had left the college classroom. It is there more than ever but in a new way. That is why the college student abandons earlier religious views.

In the American university, religion has only educational rights and privileges. If it cannot meet the tests of science, it is doomed. Its appeal to authority and revelation when subjected to objective study is found wanting. The finality of the metaphysical approach has been set aside.

Chapter Seven

The Ecclesiastical Reaction against American Higher Education

With Amendment I attached to the Constitution of the United States, the American university could not continue sectarian. Its formal theological courses were condemned to lose their dogmatic character and ultimately to vanish. Such an outcome orthodoxy had not anticipated. How could orthodox ministers be trained in liberal colleges and universities? The answer was that they could not. Hence, ecclesiastical reaction to American higher education necessarily followed three lines: The separation of the theological department from the university and its rebuilding into the sectarian seminary, the promotion of the denominational college, and the promotion of the denominational academy. To put it more bluntly, three lines of sectarian defenses had to be erected against the oncoming "godless" American educational formations. It is very noticeable that sects opposed to education during the colonial period became frenzied builders of their own educational institutions after 1790.

The American theological seminary as an independent professional school dates from the close of the eighteenth century. The "first distinctively theological institution organized in America" was that of the Reformed Church, 1784, finally located in New Brunswick in 1810. The Roman

Catholic Seminary of St. Mary was organized in Baltimore in 1791. During the first quarter of the nineteenth century eighteen seminaries representing eleven denominations were established.

The independent theological seminary offered more extensive and thorough professional training. It adapted its course of studies to the needs of the many men looking forward to the Christian ministry but unable to attend college or university. It tended to become more practical in its approach to the problems of the ministry. But it also opened a gap between the college professor and the seminary professor, between the college student and the student for the Christian ministry. It served to support denominational narrowness and promoted sectarian controversy. Its highly specialized courses prevented the layman from attending and remaining in touch with the newer theological points of view.

Bishop Westcott has pointed out how a university course tends to liberalize the minister's point of view:

Nothing can be better than that the candidate for holy orders should, whenever it is possible, enter completely and heartily into the ordinary university course—that is, that he should approach his professional study through the avenue of the liberal studies; that he should have at least the opportunity of seeing clearly the position which it holds with regard to the other branches of knowledge; that he should learn, once for all, that the truths which he has to teach, the method which he has to follow, are not antagonistic, but complementary to the truths and methods of the metaphysician and the physicist. Even if the university did no more for him than this, he could not well dispense with the teaching which places him in a true position for future work. But the Universities can do (I speak with confidence of my own University, Cambridge) far more than this. They not only reveal to the theological student the general relations in which his science stands to other sciences, but they help him to lay deeply and surely the foundations on which all later constructions may repose.

Thinking in terms of the long ago, Thwing nevertheless stated:

Theology, studied broadly, as it should be, becomes, when studied subjectively, psychology; and when studied objectively it becomes either anthropology or biology. Such a broad study of theology the university is of all institutions and agencies the best fitted to conduct. The school of theology is in peril of being a school of theology only. The results of such a narrow method cannot but be slight. For, valuing at the utmost the content of all special revelations from and concerning the divine Being, these revelations are so slight in comparison to the whole content of truth respecting God and His will that advantage must be taken of psychology, anthropology, and biology for learning whatever can be known touching Him who is the all in all.

And how inadequate the separated theological seminary is to modern requirements was indicated in *Christian Education in China* when it made the following recommendation:

The theological school shall, wherever possible, be a part of a university, being located on the same campus with the other departments, and that the students have a real share in the university life. They will thus have the advantage of the college courses and their presence will make an appeal for the ministry to the other college students. The association of the students in other departments with the students in theology, whose personality and grade of work they must respect, will have a decided influence in leading college men to consider the ministry favorably. This policy will also decrease the cost of a proper theological education by making available to the student in theology the courses in other departments of the college which are essential to his proper training.

Fortunately, the process of isolation was not completed. Harvard University in 1816 and Yale University in 1822 established divinity schools in close connection with the university. In 1836, Union Theological Seminary was founded in the interest of toleration.

It is the design of the founders to provide a theological seminary in the midst of the greatest and most growing community in America, around which all men of moderate views and feelings, who desire to live free from party strife, and to stand aloof from all extremes of doctrinal speculation, practical radicalism, and ecclesiastical domination, may cordially and affectionately rally.

Gradually "Bible Institutes" and theological seminaries have again sought contact with college and university so that at the present time there are several interdenominational seminaries, a number of non-sectarian seminaries, and numerous denominational seminaries in close affiliation with both college and university. Mutual sympathy and respect are on the increase.

At present, broadly viewed, there are four principal types of Protestant theological seminaries.

There is first of all the splendid and genuine graduate divinity school devoted to exact scholarship and original research. It is engaged in thoroughgoing study of the documents of the Old Testament and the New Testament, in discovering the true course of Christian history, the rise and development of the theology, worship, and organization of the church, and in a scientific investigation of the problems of the contemporary church. That the entire United States can boast only a few institutions of this sort is our shame. For without this relentless pursuit of Christian culture, Christianity would soon lose in educational standing and respect. The objectives of these schools are well defined. They need neither apology nor praise. They speak for themselves. Their graduates become the religious teachers of the future.

A second type of theological training is given in the large and rapidly increasing number of fundamentalist Bible schools. They also have well-defined objectives and a fixed, static, authoritarian curriculum. Their graduates minister to the millions of Protestants untouched or scarcely touched by the implications of modern culture. They have little to fear from religious liberalism as such. Their increasing menace is the gradual rise in the American cultural level and the even more Biblical cults and sects. Their losses are very considerable. A fundamentalist is no match for a cultist.

A third type of American theological seminary is the avowedly denominational school whose purpose is to train men for a distinctively denominational ministry. Here some elements of the modern culture have already been integrated with the tradition of the particular Protestant trend and therefore the religious bewilderment is less and some degree of confidence exists.

The interdenominational seminary defines its specific function to be the training of men and women for efficient Christian service in the modern environment. Here a readjustment of the curriculum to the modern environment is imperative. The purpose of the theological curriculum is the development of the Christian way of living. Since progress to be permanent must come from within, from out of the existing structure, it is safe to predict that the Christian interpretation of the future will be based upon the Christian interpretation of the present and past environment of western life.

The principal trends of the existing environment include health, conservation of natural resources, production, consumption, government, philosophy and religion, education and recreation, exchange, transportation, and communication—all interdependent and relative. The mission of the Christian church is to interpret these and synthesize them in a Christian way of life.

During the past three centuries the momentum of what is called the secularization of Christianity has steadily increased. Prior to the sixteenth century, during the period of the conquest of Christianity, the principal trends in the social order were ecclesiastical organization, the papacy, asceticism, Christian education, charity, church and state, military adventures in behalf of the church, creeds and dogmatic formulations—all authoritative, absolute, revealed.

The Christian interpretation of the future will, for a long time to come, be conditioned in part by the inherited traditional patterns. But more and more the environment of the future will accelerate the so-called process of secularization. The practice of graduating students from divinity school who are familiar only with the first meanings of the New Testament is severely criticized today and will shortly be severely condemned. The graduates of theological schools must also be able to discover permanent values in the New Testament and to articulate them with the religious needs of our contemporary life, and they must also be aware of the shortcomings of our present civilization, competent to pass stern judgment upon them and get on with the task of building the City of God. The ultimate goal of all theological education has ever been and must ever be to prepare its graduates effectively to introduce into the existing environment the leaven of love of God and neighbor.

The primary axiom of the historical study of the New

Testament has been that no passage of the New Testament can be understood unless it is studied *in situ*. To arrive at the first meaning of a statement its context must be appreciated. Thus we are at last becoming able to state definitely what the faith of Jesus was, what the Jerusalem church thought, when the death of Jesus began to be associated with salvation, how Jesus became an object of worship, why and when faith in a virgin birth originated, how the last meal and earlier meals of Jesus with his disciples were transformed into the eucharist, how Paul differed from both Jesus and John. All the recent almost marvellous reconstructions of the faith of the primitive church have developed out of this insistence upon relativity.

The most serious criticism against the New Testament curriculum of the theological seminary preparing men for the Christian ministry of today is that *all these original meanings are left hanging high in the ancient world instead of being related to the life of today*. Christian worshipers when treated to a discourse upon original meanings hang their heads in shame or bewilderment. Those first meanings mean next to nothing in their experience.

There is such a thing as history. Nineteen centuries lie between original meaning and modern meaning of a New Testament verse. Have we helped a young minister as much as we think when we have sold him a volume of original meanings? If second-century Christians no longer understood first-century Christian statements, how can we expect the miracle to occur today? New Testament study is vital for the Christian life of today only when connection is made between that life and the earliest Christian life.

Moreover, the Christian of yesterday read his new Testament differently from the Christian of today. The problem is twofold, not only historical but also psychological.

Religious truth was authoritarian, absolute, the same yesterday, today, and forever. It is becoming relative and developmental. The Christian of yesterday read his experiences back into the New Testament. He identified his experiences with those of the writers of the New Testament. He agreed with the apostles. Discrepancies, divergencies, anachronisms, contradictions did not exist for him. He had no feeling of dishonesty when he "transvaluated" the New Testament passages. Nor does the genuine fundamentalist of today. His cultural level permits him to identify the modern world view with the ancient world view without any compunctions of conscience. If difficulty arises, he is able to believe in a flat earth against all the scientists and in a man created immediately out of mud against all the evolutionists.

But the university-trained Christian of today lives in a different world from that of his grandfather. The former things have indeed passed away. All things have become new. He is aware of the existing anachronisms. He cannot employ literalism or allegorization to escape from his dilemma. If the statements in the Bible cannot be integrated with his present view of things, they fade away from his experience and no longer challenge his thought. Thus all the hard work upon the New Testament goes to waste.

From the separate theological seminary, the sects advanced to special preparatory schools, namely denominational colleges and academies where their particular trends would be cultivated. Daily chapel, days of prayer, formal courses in religion, a common table, dormitory life, personal contact with the professors would stimulate denominational interest. The curriculum was "classical"; the tuition, low; the buildings, few; the equipment, meagre; the courses, memorization of textbooks hardly alluding to modern knowledge. But the power age introduced laboratory method, necessitating the purchase of high-priced equipment which denominational colleges and academies could ill afford. Vocational training added to their troubles; the coeds preferred typewriting to theory of functions. Members of many different sects attended the same sectarian academy, compelling recognition of their presence by changes in emphasis upon denominational tenets. And how could the dance be frowned upon any longer, how could card playing and smoking be forbidden? The daughters of very pious people desired to "stay out until 1:30 A.M." Can an effective course on "immersion" be given with twenty christening groups represented in the class? Can deterioration of the faculty be avoided when orthodoxy is the top requirement and the signing of fundamentalist creeds each year is an essential? Must not the courses in "religion of any college hoping to attract a variety of students be up to the level of general intellectual life"? If four-fifths of the college students do not believe some organized religious activity vital to their religious life and substitute for it moral conduct, good citizenship, social service, public service, social and other reform, can a formal course in religion in a denominational college change the trend? The median life in the church college is not superior to that of the university and its attempt to indoctrinate American youth has not been conspicuously successful. The "piety" argument has collapsed. Without denominational subsidy, the church college will shortly pass out of American life as an ineffective educational instrument.

A midwest educator recently said:

The school which attempts to narrow the thinking of its students by indoctrinating them with particular theories in politics, economics, sociology, or religion or, what amounts to the same thing, refuses them the liberty of thought now enjoyed by the scientist, commits the unforgivable sin of making young men and women mentally old before their time, and should be classified as an academic monastery, not as an educational institution.

Specifically, the student is within his right to question the appropriateness of the halo of ethical sanctification over economic expediency or to challenge the calculated and unrelenting pursuit of profit. Adults may as individuals be pardoned for cherishing the illusion that they know what is good for the world of today. But those educators who are not part of the disease they are trying to cure are attempting to train citizens for the world of tomorrow, and only the ignorant or most presumptuous are courageous or foolish enough to predict conditions ten years hence. All we can know is that in a mutable society the oncoming generations should be always intellectually honest, courageous, sound of heart, and flexible and able of mind.

The spirit of free inquiry, the scientific attitude toward life, cannot be kept out of denominational academies and colleges and theological seminaries. It has penetrated into their most sectarian classrooms and cannot be suppressed. Charges of heresy and signing of creeds and removal of "bad" professors continue; books on evolution and social reconstruction are being culled from college libraries. But behind covers labeled Acts of the Apostles, the writings of Voltaire may be hidden. The American university has won the higher educational race. Sectarian reaction has been defeated by the scientific spirit and democratic faith.

Chapter Eight

From the "Old Deluder" Act to the Educational Policies Commission

Medieval education was under the control of the church and was not universal. Emerging humanism was not leavened by democratic ideals. Some of the great humanists of the sixteenth century escaped the anathema by avoiding the use of the vernacular. Humanism was not advocating a general levelling process. Danger lurked there.

But Protestantism was engaged in growing a new constituency. It had repudiated the traditional authority. It had enthroned the conscience of the common man. It had appealed to the Bible as final norm for thought and conduct. It had to construct a new apologetic. But how could the illiterate ordinary man read his Bible, let alone interpret it, without instruction? Protestantism looked toward the development of public education.

Within a half-dozen years after the posting of his theses, the alert Martin Luther was advocating the education of both boys and girls. Ministers had to learn Latin, Greek, and Hebrew. Gifted lads were to be sought out and trained in the classics and Hebrew so that an educated ministry might not be lacking in the church. Two centuries and one-half before America paid attention to the education of girls, Luther insisted that money be taken from the common fund to provide for the instruction of girls under twelve years of age in the Christian way of life and in reading and writing German. Seven years later Luther again pointed out that the purity of the gospel could be maintained only if good schools for both boys and girls were opened and developed. As early as 1524, he began to emphasize that popular schools had a twofold purpose, a civic purpose as well as a religious purpose, and that the state had a stake in education. In his "letter to the magistrates of all the cities of Germany in behalf of Christian schools," he pointed out that competent officials can be grown only in schools established by the state for all boys and girls. In 1530 Luther preached a rather long "sermon on the duty of sending children to school" and held that the state ought to compel its citizens to send their children to school. Education should be compulsory, at least for children considering the ministry, law, pastorate, teaching, medicine, or a political career. Thus, through primary schools employing German, secondary schools employing Latin, and the university, Luther hoped that Lutheranism would survive.

Universal literacy was a fundamental with John Calvin. George Bancroft has called him "the father of popular education, the inventor of the system of free schools." But it was the church which had to provide schools in such quantity that all might learn to read. *The schoolteacher under Calvinism was a church official.* As early as 1538, Calvin proposed an elementary school in the vernacular for all in Geneva. His secondary school, or college, was sharply differentiated from the university. The Bible was studied. But this meant the acquisition of Hebrew as well as of Latin and Greek. Hebrew led to other Oriental languages. The fauna and flora of Palestine, its mineralogy and geography and history, invited attention. Thus Calvinism was building the bridge into the scientific era. Interest in source material, development in critical attitude, ability to interpret, and capacity for appreciation issued from this intense study of the Bible.

Wherever Calvinism appeared, schools were fostered. *By the end of the sixteenth century the Netherlands had flourishing public schools.* The Great Synod of Dort, 1618, even ordered that the children of the poor should be instructed *gratuitously.* Gradually school taxes were levied. In 1629 the West India company ordered that Dutch colonists on Manhattan "shall endeavor to find out ways and means whereby they may supply a minister and a schoolmaster." The Dutch public school fostered liberty.

Various dissenting English groups came to Massachusetts in the seventeenth century to perpetuate their religion. One of these bodies established the Massachusetts bibliocracy and wedded education to religion. It exhorted the heads of all the families to nurture the religious life. But the fire on many family altars went out. The Christian home was not providing the necessary training in faith and morals. So the Puritans resorted to law. In 1642, the General Court "ordered that the Selectmen of every Town . . . shall have a vigilant eye over their brethren and neighbors, to see, First that none of them shall suffer so much Barbarism in any of their families, as not to endeavor to teach, by themselves or others, their children and apprentices so much learning, as may enable them perfectly to read the English tongue and knowledge of the Capital Lawes; upon penalty of 20 schillings for each neglect therein."

Five years later came the history-making enactment which begins, "It being one chief project of that old deluder, Satan, to keep men from the knowledge of the Scriptures, as in former times by keeping them in an unknown tongue, so in these latter times, by persuading from the use of tongues (that so at least the true sense and meaning of the original must be clouded by false glosses of saint-seeming deceivers), that learning may not be buried in the grave of our fathers in the church and commonwealth, the Lord assisting our endeavors," and orders the education of all children at private or public cost. These Massachusetts laws "embodied in large measure the principles of public education" afterward developed in the constitutions of the forty-eight states.

During the colonial age, American education had a very specific religious purpose, and ecclesiastical control was exerted over curriculum, pupils, and teachers. In New England, the "compulsory maintenance attitude" was introduced; in the middle colonies, the parochial school attitude prevailed; in the southern colonies there were private schools for the wealthy and charity schools for the poor.

In the early decades of nationhood, the struggle for free public schools was intense with the "old aristocratic and conservative elements, rural residents and taxpayers, sectarians like Lutherans and Quakers, private school proprietors, Southerners and non-English speaking residents" opposing their introduction, and "democratic leaders, philanthropists and humanitarians, city residents and non-taxpayers, Calvinists and citizens of New England, working men, propaganda societies" favoring them. The fight for the state's right to tax for the support of public education was won by 1850. The pauper-school idea and pro-rated tuitions very slowly succumbed. Finally, sectarianism yielded to the American ideal of free schools for all children at public cost. The ecclesiastical interpretation of public education had not been able to overcome the functional interpretation demanded by the American way of life. "The free school is the promoter of that intelligence which is to save us." Patriotism and intelligence have stood up well against superstition and ignorance. As Supreme Court Justice Frank Murphy recently wrote:

From the earliest days, America has stood for these affirmative values:

First, a passionate love of freedom, an eternal hostility

against every form of tyranny over the mind of man.

Second, a concern for the value and dignity of the common man based upon an intense desire for equality of opportunity. The mainspring of American civilization is this dignity of each one in daily existence.

Third, kindliness and good will toward others. One of the deepest sources for this distinctive American trait is the tradition within most families of the privation and sufferings of their forebears before they left the old world and were safely settled in the new.

Fourth, an immense confidence in the creative energies of man. This arises from each American's own experience and the tradition of American practicality, inventiveness, strength, energy and exuberant spirit.

Fifth, a keen sense of the interdependence of all Americans, of the necessity for teamwork, of the manifold values of good fellowship.

We Americans are proud of being individualistic in the sense of being self-reliant. Yet from earliest pioneer days we have also practiced cooperation.

These are the values that created public education and will preserve it for the oncoming generations.

Merritt Thompson has summarized John Dewey's philosophy of education thus:

The public school is the chief means of social betterment. The ideal school is a miniature society. The aim of education is social efficiency; utilization rather than subordination of the capacities of the individual. It takes place by participation, is life not a preparation for life. Its means are: play, construction, use of tools, contact with nature, expression and activity. The school is social environment: simplified, purified, balanced, and graded. Its goal is cooperation and mutually helpful living. Learning takes place by doing; originality and initiative are the chief virtues of the school to be cultivated as against obedience and submission. The school prepares for political life by giving pupils opportunity for exercise of responsibility and social insight in school. Educational bases are psychological and sociological. Personality is achieved. The method of education is the reconstruction of experience. Intelligence is the purposive reorganization of experience. Education is the means of social continuity.

Public education has indeed put many miles between it and its predecessor:

> "In Adam's fall
> We sinned all."

> "I in the burying place may see
> Graves shorter there than I;
> From death's arrest no age is free,
> Young children too may die."

John Cotton's *Spiritual Milk for American Babes Drawn Out of the Breasts of Both Testaments for Their Souls' Nourishment* is not a textbook today and non-elect infants are no longer allocated to "the easiest room in hell." Obstinate and unruly children can no longer legally be put to death. Religious terrorism is not resorted to in public schools to "train children in the way of the Lord." "Schools are mutual grounds with children of all denominations in attendance." The non-Christian child has equal rights in the American public school classroom with the Christian child. As Cora Heineman has put it: "So far as I know, the American system of free public schools is the only public institution in history to be founded on the principle of the brotherhood of man as he is."

Chapter Nine

The Ecclesiastical Reaction against American Public Education

Both Protestantism and Catholicism opposed the development of public education in the United States by promoting the parochial school. The puny efforts of the Protestant groups soon came to grief and what remains of the Protestant parochial school today has little meaning for American youth. The Roman Catholic parochial school, however, persistently criticizes public education and claims ethical and religious superiority.

Modern Vatican pronouncements upon education are numerous. Leo XIII in *Inscrutabili*, 1878, defined the three fundamental Catholic obligations to be loyalty to Rome, or subordination to the Holy See, religious education, and the Catholic ideal of marriage and family life. Religious education "should be wholly in harmony with the Catholic Faith in its literature and system of training and chiefly in philosophy, upon which the foundation of the other sciences in great measure depends." *

In *Immortale Dei*, 1885, Leo XIII listed the four leading errors of contemporary life as: 1. "The sovereignty of the people . . . is held to reside in the multitude. . . . Princes

* A convenient summary of papal deliverances in Philip Hughes, *The Popes' New Order* (New York, 1944).

are nothing more than delegates chosen to carry out the will
of the people"; 2. All religions are equally good or true;
this is the "same thing as atheism"; 3. There should be un-
restricted freedom of thought and the right to publish it;
4. The church should be subject to the state in the exercise
of its duty. In discussing errors one and three particularly,
the Pope criticizes the American way of life.

In *Militantis Ecclesiae*, 1897, Leo XIII wrote: "What is
needed is not only that religious instruction should be given
to the young people at certain fixed times, but with the
spirit of Christian piety. If this is wanting, if this sacred
atmosphere does not pervade and warm the hearts of masters
and scholars alike, little good can be expected from any
kind of learning, and considerable harm will often be the
consequence. . . . The mere fact that a school gives some
religious instruction . . . does not . . . make it a fit place
for Catholic pupils."

In *Ubi Arcano Dei*, 1922, Pius XI enumerates the three
instances of contemporary apostasy from God as: 1. The
people as source of the state's authority; 2. Marriage regarded as a civil contract; 3. "God and Jesus Christ were
banished from the education of the young . . . so that
children came to think that in their lives no importance
need be attached to religion and to God, as either no mention was ever made of them or, if spoken of, it was in words
full of contempt." The first two are, however, fundamentals
of American democracy while the third, if it refers to
American public education, is caricature.

In *Divini Illius Magistri*, 1931, Pius XI defined the
Catholic school as one in which "all the teaching and the
whole organization of the school, its teachers, syllabus, textbooks of every kind are regulated by the Catholic spirit,
under the direction and supervision of the Church." In
countries of different religious beliefs the state ought "to
leave free scope to the initiative of the Church and of the

family to organise schools *while giving them such assistance as justice demands.*" The true product of Catholic education is "the supernatural man . . . [who] thinks, judges and acts constantly and consistently in accordance with right reason illumined by the supernatural light of the example and teaching of Christ."

In *Summi Pontificatus*, 1939, Pius XII held that any "training of the young which of deliberate purpose neglects to direct their minds also toward that fatherland which is heaven does a grave wrong. . . . Such secular education may seem . . . a source of hardihood and vigor . . . but . . . any training of young minds which neglects or repudiates the feeling and spirit of the Christian [Catholic] religion is a crime of high treason against Him who is King of Kings and Lord of Lords . . . [and] is destined to reap a bitter harvest."

According to the Vatican, then, the purpose of education is intellectual, moral, and religious with the Roman Catholic religion the centre of the system. The dogmas of the Catholic faith, the precepts of the Divine Law as understood by Catholicism must be taught and practical training given in prayer, in attendance upon divine worship, and in the seven sacraments.

But public education departs from the old philosophical terminology and emphasizes human needs—health, family life, economic adjustment, civic life, recreation, and ethical religion. Thus the conflict with the parochial school kind of education cannot be avoided.

How inevitable this collision is, the very popular writer in English and American Catholic circles, Hilaire Belloc, shows in *The Contrast* and in two magazine articles.* There is a "necessary conflict," he writes, "between the civil state and the Catholic Church where the two are not identified."

* *The Century Magazine*, April, 1924, pp. 824ff.; *The Catholic World*, CXIX, 1924, p. 742.

The Catholic Church is in its root principle at issue with the civic definition both of freedom and authority. For the purpose of the state, religion is either a universally admitted system or a matter of individual choice.

But by the definition which is the very soul of Catholicism, religion must be for the Catholic, first, a supreme authority, superior to any claims of the state; secondly, a corporate thing, and not an individual thing; thirdly, a thing dependent upon authority, and not upon a personal mood; fourthly, a guarantee of individual freedom in all that is not of the faith.

Catholic culture must in its very nature be, in the long run, either supreme or persecuted in any society. . . . In a predominantly Catholic society, the secret societies which are native to anti-Catholic countries would be suppressed. The morals of anti-Catholic society, as expressed in its literature, would not be tolerated. Its moral tendencies (as, for instance, what is called "eugenics") would in a mainly Catholic society be punished as criminal.

Now the culture of the United States is from its original religion and by its momentum and whole tradition, opposed to the Catholic Church. The Catholic Church is not one sect out of many which can all agree to live in amity, because they are no more than opinions. It is the one thing on earth which is most completely individual. It is a personality and in proportion as that personality is recognized and begins to produce its manifold effects, *it challenges all things different and opposed to itself.*

While Belloc reflects the European theoretical and dogmatic Catholic point of view, there has been much American Catholic dissent to it. Here there have always been those who have been for understanding and co-operation. Monsignor George Johnson, for example, is quoted as having recently said: "Public education will have to face and solve the problem of religious and moral instruction. We shall have to help in this respect. . . . These demands may revolutionize our teaching in religion. . . . The relations of church and state in respect to education may also have to be rethought in the light of post-war conditions. The old question of federal aid will have to be settled and perhaps our traditional stand altered."

In *The Vatican and the War*, Camille Cianfarra points out that "the individual today often feels that he is first a citizen and then a Catholic." He prefers sometimes the welfare of his country at war to that of his Church. Because there were Catholics in all the nations at war, the Vatican could not condemn any group without risking Catholic repercussions in another.

Isaac Hecker of Paulist Father fame once commented: "Americans do not want the Pope, at the head of the most august assembly in the world, representing the whole Christian Church, to speak in favor of empires, monarchies, or republics: that we do not want. . . . It is an error radical and gross to say that the basis of the American character is the spirit of political and religious rebellion. . . . We do not need the imperial or kingly ideas of the Old World as aids to our spiritual life as Catholics, any more than we want its anarchical ideas as helps to civil freedom as citizens."

Archbishop Ireland outlined his political creed thus: "To priest, to bishop, to Pope, who . . . should attempt to rule in matters civil and political, to influence the citizen beyond the range of their own orbit of jurisdiction . . . the answer is quickly made: 'Back to your own sphere of rights and duties—back to the things of God!'"

And American Catholic homes in great numbers are represented not only in the public schools but in the management and teaching personnel. The Catholic public school teachers and principals do not relish the adjective in the epithet "godless public schools."

Pamphlets like *May an American Oppose the Public Schools?* by Paul L. Blakely with its "our first duty to the public school is not to pay taxes for its maintenance. . . . The first duty of every Catholic father to the public school is to keep his children out of it," and books like *Our National Enemy Number One, Education without Religion* by John F. Noll, apparently a Roman Catholic bishop, are making many Americans very weary of hearing about the religio-ethical superiority of church schools. For them Genesis is no longer a sourcebook on race theory nor Gury's *Casus Conscientiae* a textbook on ethics nor the item on the "relics of the passion" (*National Catholic Almanac*, 1945, page 238) history.

How undemocratic it would be for the state to finance church schools appears from the resulting advantages to such schools: 1. Escape from direct democratic control over these schools; 2. Right to impose their religious tests on teachers; 3. The promotion of their doctrines under their own censorship; 4. Ownership of their schools; 5. Retention of their general voting rights and privileges in public school matters, according to Arvid J. Burke.*

In the Louisiana textbook case, the United States Supreme Court held that if private school pupils enjoy free textbooks by state grant, they must be "the same as those furnished for public schools and not religious or sectarian in character."

Dr. Mordecai Grossman opposes the provided parochial school:

> . . . The parochial school is likely to fashion an indoctrinated mentality incapable of coping with the problems of a world in the throes of revolutionary change. All institutional religions, the Jewish religion included, have

* In his *Defensible Spending for Public Schools* (New York, 1943), p. 207.

their bases in beliefs in the supernatural. Beliefs in the supernatural may have their utility in motivating the good life, in giving the good life the quality of sanctity. But they cannot tell us what the good life is. The good way of life must be formulated on the basis of natural experiences and of people studying, living, and working together. There is no Jewish, no Catholic, no Protestant solution to the problems of creating a more peaceful, more just, and saner world. There is only a human solution—a solution to be discovered by all the peoples cooperatively. Jewish supernaturalism, as Christian supernaturalism, is only likely to be a divisive, not a unifying force. There can be no agreement on theological propositions because there is no way of proving or refuting any of them. Should we approach the practical problems of society from the points of view of our different theologies, we should wind up with confusion worse confounded. Let the churches and synagogues encourage the cooperative human quest for a better way of life, let them sanctify the best that the human mind and the human heart can attain. But it would not be wise to surrender to them the exclusive responsibility of fashioning the human mind.

American Catholicism has various ways of providing religious instruction for its youth. It has Sunday Schools, vacation schools, released time schools, and parochial schools. Its Sunday School enrollment decreased from 1,860,836 in 1916 to 972,891 in 1936—a decline of 47.7 per cent in two decades. The Official Catholic Directory, 1945, listed 638,-484 "pupils attending Roman Catholic Vacation Schools" in 1944. This was excellent progress. The principal method of Catholic religious instruction has been the parochial school which has yet to reach the half-way mark of its 5–17 age group.

How did Roman Catholicism become interested in released time, the practice of releasing children from school for religious instruction? Some five years ago in his brilliant article upon "The Conflict among Catholics" in *The American Scholar*, George N. Shuster stated that the mass demand for higher learning after World War I "could not be met by any private agency no matter how generously supported. Unavoidably large numbers of Catholic young people had to go to secular institutions for advanced study. . . . The Church was acutely aware of the almost universal drift to indifference, moral laxity, and philosophical skepticism. *Realizing that segregation was impossible, wide-awake [Catholic] leaders started a movement to foster religious instruction in public schools.* The critics may say this effort was belated and that it was conducted without a great deal of insight into the psychology of public relations. But though there may be some truth in the charge, one can hardly deny that Catholic fears were in large measure legitimate." This is eloquent testimony to the failure of the parochial school to meet earlier hopes for it.

How successful has the Roman Catholic released time experiment been? The 1936 United States Census of Religious Bodies for the first time provided an over-all picture of the released time situation here. It reports on 256 different bodies, merely enumerates or refers to some 60 other such groups, and has probably skipped enough to bring United States religious bodies to a grand total of 350.

One hundred and thirty of the 256 listed groups are reported as having no interest in the plan. Two-thirds of the dismissed-time pupils come from Roman Catholic, Adventist, and Lutheran bodies. The proportion of the 5 to 17 age United States population reported enrolled in weekday religious schools comes to 3.63 per cent, with Catholicism contributing 52.7 per cent and Lutheranism 13.7 per cent. Other Protestant groups contribute 23.4 per cent, Jewish congregations 7.4 per cent, and the cults 2.8 per cent. Yet the Roman Catholic ratio of United States population in 1936 came to only 15.5 per cent and over 40 per cent of its youth attended Catholic schools.

Selecting 22 representative Protestant "families" accounting for most of the United States Protestant population, we obtain the following line-up of interest: Lutheran, Churches of God, Mennonites, Plymouth Brethren, Adventists, Presbyterians, Evangelical and Reformed, Evangelical, Assemblies of God, Moravians, Federated Churches, Congregational and Christian Churches, Methodists, Disciples, Church of the Nazarene, Baptists, United Brethren, Church of the Brethren, Protestant Episcopal, Churches of Christ, Universalists, and Unitarians. The range of interest is from the Lutheran high of 3.6 per cent to the Unitarian low of practically zero, with the bulk of the Protestant population less than .9 per cent.

The Catholic interest varies from the Polish National Catholic Church high of 5.6 per cent to the Old Catholic Bodies low of zero with the Eastern Orthodox Churches at 3.4 per cent and Roman Catholicism at 2.9 per cent.

The Jewish Congregations' interest is 1.8 per cent. The American Ethical Union interest is zero.

While the Salvation Army interest is 4.7 per cent, that of the Volunteers is zero. The American religious cults vary from the Latter Day Saints high of 4 per cent to the Church of Christ Scientist low of approximately zero, with Spiritualism at 2.1 per cent. The Vedanta Society's interest comes to 3.9 per cent and the Buddhist Mission's to 1 per cent.

Nationally viewed, by 1936, the trend in the released time experiment was greatly favoring Catholicism.

Only two local situations will be sampled. In New York City the 80 per cent Catholic enrollment in weekday church schools of 1943 became 81.43 per cent as of 1945. In the promotional literature of the weekday church school, Rochester, New York, is generously advertised as "the first city in New York State to undertake city-wide weekday church schools on released time."

Since the Protestant weekday church school has been ably cultivated for almost a quarter of a century in such fertile soil as Rochester and has of late been unified under the jurisdiction of the local federation of churches, a survey of its present progress ought to indicate the standing of the national experiment some years hence.

Statistics are available for the Rochester dismissed time experiment during the past five years. Of 24,173 pupils in elementary schools in November, 1940, 8,167, or 33.8 per cent, were released for weekday religious education. Of these, 66.9 per cent were Catholic and 33 per cent Protestant. Of 20,408 pupils in elementary schools four years later, 6,895, or 33.7 per cent, were released for weekday religious education. Of these, 66.1 per cent were Catholic and 33.5 per cent Protestant. In the November, 1945, report the Catholic percentage was 65.3 and the Protestant 34.5. The elementary school dismissed time situation in Rochester appears stabilized with twice as many Catholic students released as Protestants, although the non-Catholic elementary school student ratio to Catholic is more than three to one.

Of 18,071 pupils in Rochester public high schools in September, 1941, 5,217, or 28.8 per cent, were on a dismissed time basis. Of these 80.8 per cent were Catholic, and 17.5 per cent Protestant. Of 14,101 pupils in Rochester public high schools in October, 1944, 3,525, or 24.2 per cent, were on a dismissed time basis. Of these 82.3 per cent were Catholic, and 15.2 per cent Protestant. Of 13,638 pupils in Rochester high schools in October, 1945, 3,833, or 28.1 per cent, were on the dismissed time basis. Of these 83.0 per cent were Catholic, 13.7 per cent were Protestant, and 3.1 per cent were Jewish. Between 1941 and 1945 the Protestant percentage of released time pupils in Rochester high schools decreased 3.8 per cent and the Catholic percentage increased 2.2 per cent. There were more than five times as many Catholic released time students in Rochester high schools in 1944 as Protestants—in 1945, more than six times as many: 3,183 compared with 526. And yet, in Rochester, the Catholic public high school students are outnumbered about four to one by non-Catholic students. By 1960, Protestant interest in high school released time in Rochester, N. Y., will drop to zero at the present rate of retardation.

After all this intensified effort on the part of American Catholicism to provide Catholic education for Catholic youth, the total number of Roman Catholic students under direct and indirect Catholic religious instruction in 1944 was reported officially to be 3,205,864. Hence, it seems that well over one million American Roman Catholic children 5 to 17 years of age do not receive formal Catholic religious education.

In Missouri, the Supreme Court unanimously held that "the inclusion of a parochial school in the public school system constitutes a denial of the guarantee of religious freedom," declaring:

The constitutional policy of our state has decreed the absolute separation of church and state, not only in governmental matters but in educational ones as well. Public money, coming from taxpayers of every denomination, may not be used for the help of any religious sect in education or otherwise. If the management of this school were approved, we might next have some other church gaining control of a school board and have its pastor and teachers introduced to teach its sectarian religion. Our schools would soon become the centers of local political battles which would be dangerous to the peace of society, where there must be equal religious rights to all and special privileges to none.

The Missouri Court also found that "any religious instruction, even if only inferred by symbols or the segregation of pupils into denominational groups, automatically prevents a school from receiving public money."

Neither the Protestant nor the Catholic parochial school system has been able to shake the faith of the American people in its educational system. The public school, far from being "godless," has merely been making the necessary religious adjustments to keep in step with developing American life. The public school from the functional point of view is doing infinitely more for intelligent religion than the various types of formal religious education.

Chapter Ten

The Released Time Experiment

The religious training of the American child became an acute problem for Protestantism early in the twentieth century. But public schools could not be transformed into sectarian schools. The battle against sectarianism had been won by the public schools. Against the reintroduction of formal religious instruction into the public schools were not only the provisions of the Constitution of the United States and hundreds of Court decisions but also the existence of over three hundred divergent American religious bodies and the fact that a majority of the population was not affiliated with the churches. Moreover, Protestant attendance upon worship services was quite spotty.

If the public schools could not be converted into Protestant schools, could not Protestant and non-church-going students in the public schools be excused for Protestant instruction under Protestant teachers in Protestant churches? *What the "heathen" majority might do never occurred to the proponents of this plan. Suppose non-church-going parents organize weekday schools for the inculcation of liberal interpretations of modern life? Suppose they insist upon propagating their religious points of view?* What a bedlam the United States will become! To meet the emergency, a modified Gary Plan was proposed. Turn time off from the long hours imposed upon young and old, hitherto used for appreciation of music and books, enjoyment of tennis, swimming, shows, dancing, into the enjoyment of religious education. It was so ordered.

After three decades of propaganda in behalf of the weekday "church school," can the plan be called a success? Or is there a case for the American way of life as over against released time? Is released time doing injury to the students, to the churches themselves, to the cardinal American principle of separation of church and state, to public education? Are the admittedly good intentions of its advocates an offset to the permanent damage resulting for the American way?

There are many reasons which make the released time experiment of doubtful value. Only a few may be examined here. We must omit for lack of space such arguments as the claim that the released time plan is testimony to the inadequacy of the Sunday School to meet the religious needs of the twentieth century; released time is causing the further disintegration of the Sunday School; released time is an entering wedge for the introduction of sectarianism into public education; released time is a method of taking a religious census. The case for the American way which is antithetical to released time is summarized in only fifteen points of which the last four are principal.*

* The materials of this chapter were derived from correspondence, reports of associations, magazine articles, and so on. Among the principal sources are: *The Weekday Church School in New York State*, Rev. 1941, Albany; *The Weekday Church School*, Int. Council, Chicago, 1940; United States *Census of Religious Bodies*, 1936; Annual Reports WDREA, Rochester Federation of Churches; Annual Reports, The Public Education Association, New York City; State of New York Law Pamphlet 6, *Use of School Buildings*; *The National Catholic Almanac*, esp. 1943 and 1945; *The Official Catholic Directory*, various years; *The Nation's Schools*, espec. recent years; *Scottish Rite News Bulletin*, espec. 1943 to 1945; *Catholic Herald Citizen*, Milwaukee, August 26, 1944; H. M. Kallen, *Religious Education in Democratic Society*; E. L. Thorndike, *Your City*; S. S. Wyer, *Specifications for Religion for Democracy*; V. T. Thayer, *American Education under Fire*; Arvid J. Burke, *Defensible Spending for Public Schools*; Conrad H. Moehlman, *School and Church: The American Way*.

1. *The student reaction to the released time proposal has not been very favorable.*

One public school teacher writes: "I have a hard time keeping those already registered going. One after another comes in with this or that excuse which they try again next week if it works this week. Since part of the grade remains in school, the problem is what to do with them. Regular work cannot be carried on because those that need it most are taking religion. It is one long headache. Another bad feature is that the Protestant children return fifteen minutes earlier than the Catholic children. If the priest has something special on at the church the Catholic children don't go at all but regard regular school work for the period as 'punishment.' Some take the attitude, 'Well, I'm done with the church for this week, now I don't have to go to Sunday School.' Disunity between Catholic and Protestant children is increased by dismissed time. My experience has been that the plan has little value."

A released time teacher put it this way: "If a vote were to be taken as to whether Religious Education should be a part of the effort of the public schools from the sixth grade through the twelfth, my 'nay' would be louder than all the rest. . . . The chapter on 'Can the Bible Return to the Classroom' provoked such side-splitting laughter that I had to wash the tears from my glasses before I could read further. In my experience 'released time' is nothing more than an excuse for those who attend to get away from their jail for an hour, and how the sophisticated Veronica Lakes and Clark Gables are horrified and shocked when they happen to stumble upon a teacher in a 'religion class' that expects a little evidence of energy and grey matter on their part."

Where credit is given for released time activities, only a small minority of students often ask for it according to statements by superintendents of schools. Could student judgment as to the value of the released time curriculum and teachers be more effectively registered?

A competent Pennsylvania minister is not in doubt: ". . . This present drive for religion in the schools is a blind alley; . . . in one high school of 2,500 students, 40 were enrolled and of those not one teacher or one pupil was satisfied with it."

2. *The democracy of the public school campus and classroom is disintegrating.*

From the earliest period of American life to the present moment there has been religious strife here. All the religious animosities of Europe were transported hither. Protestant still fears Catholic, and Catholic, Protestant. Baptist opposes Baptist, and Plymouth Brethren I, Plymouth Brethren VI.

In spite of all this religious hatred, a miracle was wrought in the course of the nineteenth century by public education. The youthful representatives of the various races and creeds sat side by side in the same classrooms unconscious of the antagonistic attitudes of their elders. As a result, when these boys and girls became men and women, they joined the same churches and gave us our cross-sectional northern Protestantism. In many larger "denominational" churches, a dozen denominations may be represented. The native American laity has become indifferent to particular denominational tenets. This is very wholesome.

When procedure to line up the youngsters for their "religion" classes segregates Americans as Catholics, Lutherans, other Protestants, Jews, cultists, smaller sects, non-church-going pupils, a consciousness of religious cleavage is inevitable and it is baneful.

Is not local religious divisiveness accentuated by the sight of public school children united upon the campus and in the classroom walking in different directions to their respective sectarian schools? When the separate denominations conduct their sectarian propaganda within different rooms in the same school, the only conclusion the children can draw is that there is unity in every other phase of American life with the exception of religion. The area of religion must continue even in the twentieth century to be an arena of conflict; "divided we listen to Father, Pastor, layworker." And the great majority of the children of America who remain in their classrooms become "atheists" for the religious absentees.

3. *The average American views released time as a confession of weakness and failure on the part of the American churches.*

With after-school hours, Saturday, Sunday, and evening hours at their disposal, churches dare to ask for a portion of school time and indirectly involve the state in financial support of their denominationalism. Some one is footing that bill! But Johnny will not attend a class in religion after school hours. Precisely, the churches must use the bait of release from attendance upon public school to compel him through home and other pressures to go along with the procession. It is the "only way by which one-half of the children of this district will ever get any religious training at all." Of 20,000 religiously neglected children in Rochester, New York, the local federation of churches reported "349" reached by its weekday "Church School" a couple of years ago. That was about 1.7 per cent. But granting the claim, can a more tragic admission of failure by the churches in religious education be imagined? Whenever the churches lean back upon the state to rescue them from their own problems, they depreciate themselves until their autonomy finally vanishes. Consider Europe.

4. *The released time experiment witnesses to the conflict within Protestantism between religious education and the Sunday School.*

The argument for the weekday church school as over

against the Sunday School is thus boldly stated in the literature of the released time experiment:

> In many communities the weekday school is education-
> ally far more efficient than the Sunday School and other
> teaching agencies of the church. Among the reasons for
> this, the following may be mentioned:
>
> 1. A quality of teaching comparable with the best in
> public schools has been frequently brought about by in-
> sistence on the part of public school authorities.
>
> 2. Because teachers are paid (as is quite common in
> weekday schools), the churches can demand proper
> training and thorough preparation for each session. Fre-
> quently, therefore, children get better teachers—at least
> as good as public school teachers.
>
> 3. There is more regularity. The matter of poor clothes
> does not keep children away. Neither does bad weather,
> indifference, indisposition, auto rides, or parties.
>
> 4. There is punctuality, partly because of less inter-
> ference by other engagements.
>
> 5. The mind of the child is more teachable because of
> association with public school on week days. It is part of
> the regular educational program and part of school life.

Maybe this style of argument is not injurious to the Sunday School, but some day mother may agree with dad: "The
Sunday School is an affliction our Tommie need no longer
endure."

5. *There are two interpretations of the released time
experiment by its promoters, predicting schism a little later
on.*

Sectarian Protestantism has no interest in a weekday
church school which does not perpetuate its dogma. But the
liberal advocates of the weekday church school plan certainly do not have any such objective. Harrison Elliott, for
example, has consistently contended that "fundamentalist

procedure and true education are not compatible." He holds that "there are two ways in which you can look at religious education. One aspect is its understanding and appreciation. . . . The other is one's personal religious faith and personal religious affiliation. *That is bound to be sectarian.* . . . Personal religious faith and affiliation are always a sectarian matter in the true sense of that term. . . . *I cannot see how it is possible for the public school to provide this aspect of religion.*"

What a religious tug-of-war will ensue when Fundamentalism finally detects the intentions of the liberals to substitute the historical study of the Bible for its "revelation" and its "verbally inspired Bible"! Sectarianism "caused the exclusion" of the formal teaching of religion from public education in the first place. When this approaching seven years' war is over, religion in the United States will have become really democratic. Resentment of the majority of Americans over this indirect attempt to make it pay for sectarian Bible teaching will not recede.

And the Sunday School, in spite of its inefficiencies and religious illiteracy and inability to meet the religious needs of the twentieth century, is bound to fight against its complete disintegration by the "superior curriculum and personnel" of the weekday church school. When the traditional Sunday School awakens to the risks to orthodoxy in the objectives of the liberals in the weekday church school plan, its leaders will hold enthusiastic mass conventions against the sponsors of Sunday School conventions that of late years have become "coldly intellectual and professional gatherings in which the laity have been noticeably absent."

Not only will the released time plan be opposed by non-church-going Americans—the great majority, by the conservative promoters of the traditional Sunday School, by denominationalists, sects, and cults now supporting it, but it contains within itself the seeds of dissolution. As for leaders who "desire to introduce a sort of non-sectarian ethical religious teaching into the regular public school curriculum," here is a liberal analysis of such a plan: ". . . while the most important aspect of religious teaching is its ethical ideal, that ethical ideal cannot be effectively segregated from the background of the religion as a culture. What we lack is not the recognition of an ethical philosophy of life, but the means of implementing it by a truly effective ethical way of life which grows out of a distinctive tradition and heritage."

6. *Released time on ministers and ministers on released time.*

When "highbrow" religious education failed of adoption by the American Sunday School, its discouraged Protestant promoters seem to have turned to the released time plan not only to secure another opportunity to elevate the curriculum of the traditional Sunday School but also to eliminate the troublemaking orthodox, not to say fundamentalist, ministers who had so effectively resisted the introduction of revised religious education into the Sunday School. Else why do the weekday church school promotional pamphlets contain items like these: "For many years, untrained though devoted folk in every community have given themselves to the task of teaching religion in the Sunday School. They deserve great credit for what they have done. The world would be much poorer if it were not for their labors. However, in this twentieth century, with its knowledge of the laws of learning and with its need of a vital religion, the religious educator finds that his task has been immensely increased. He needs deep and rich resources as he seeks to teach a religion which will give meaning and direction and motive to life." The sectarian teaching of the Sunday School must go. "The basic truths of religion must function in life —reverence for God, truth, love, service, purity, honesty, and tolerance." "Often the whole environment of the public

school is so much more attractive than the church environment that children choose to go to the weekday school
whereas they are not attracted to the Sunday School."

Or this verdict upon the ministers:

Let us be realistic. Probably in the large majority of
communities, it will be necessary for a minister to serve
as supervisor. Two questions immediately arise:

1. How can a minister find the time with all his other
duties? It becomes virtually a matter of the relative importance of the various activities engaging a minister's
time and energies. That it is possible for him to devote
a larger portion of his time to educational work is at-
tested by the fact that many ministers are now functioning efficiently as supervisors, both in their local parishes
and in community enterprises.

2. Is a minister trained to supervise an educational
program? There is an increasing number of ministers who
have had training for educational leadership in college,
state, and normal schools, theological seminaries, and
schools of religious education. They have had courses in
educational psychology, educational philosophy, and educational techniques. *A large percentage, however, have
entered their career without technical preparation for such
leadership. Many such have, through graduate courses in
education and through private study, equipped themselves
for supervising an educational program.*

In "Standards for New York State Weekday Church
Schools," the formal educational background required of
leaders is described as to minimum: "College or Normal
School Graduation, or their equivalent, special training in
Bible and Religious Education"; as to "highly desirable":
"equivalent of public school teacher of parallel grade." Then
this parenthesis upon the clergy: "Ministers should be expected to fulfill same requirements, particularly in pecul-

iarly educational preparation. Those now teaching should be strongly urged to meet the minimum requirements"!

This next reference to ministers is a bit more polite: "Don't depend too much upon ministers to do the teaching; with the finest spirit of sacrificial service most ministers are too burdened with pastoral duties to give to this task the time and effort it requires." Those busy ministers who can only teach catechism and refuse to read the provided textbooks!

In the released time plan in Kentucky, clergymen are not to teach classes in religion "because they do not usually have the technical training which is necessary for securing a certificate to teach children in the grades." And when these children listen to their ministers the following Sunday, are they supposed to rise in revolt against their antiquated message?

Ministers in ever greater numbers are opposing released time programs. Thus a New York State pastor describes released time: "As in so many places, religious education is being tried here on the 'released time' basis. The Congregational minister is using the hour to present the bases for church membership to a small group of his students. The Advent-Christian minister preaches to his even smaller number. The Methodist minister meets his young people in the same fashion. When the matter came up before my own Board of Deacons, I stated my own position in terms of the argument you have so ably set forth in your book.* There was not a single dissenting voice when I asked for an informal vote. Consequently, the Baptist boys and girls are kept under school discipline during the hour."

7. *Does the released time experiment promote Protestant unity?*

The religious disunity of the proponents of dismissed time plans is one of the principal arguments against released time.

* *School and Church: The American Way.*

Released time not only divides public school students into four major groups: Catholics, Protestants, Jews, and the majority or minority that remains behind in the classrooms, but it also breaks up Protestant withdrawers into separate "armies of the Lord"; liberal Protestant against fundamentalist Protestant, cultist against sectarian enthusiast, Lutheran against Baptist. When weekday church school sessions are held in schoolrooms, they often become catechism against catechism.

8. *Does the released time experiment promote Catholic-Protestant understanding?*

The President of Hunter College, George N. Shuster, just back from a trip to Germany, reported that "in discussing the future political organization of Germany, Catholics uniformly said that *they wished to make common cause with their Protestant brethren.* Both sides have suffered terribly, and what little consolation they have is found in the fact that the Christian faith has its martyrs, to be remembered as heroes and cherished as exemplars of conduct." There will be interfaith co-operation in Germany hereafter.

Will it extend to the educational system? No! Catholics and Protestants must have separate schools. "For example," continued President Shuster, "the Archbishop of Cologne stressed the fact, in his Pastoral Letter, that letting Catholics and Protestants have separate schools was more likely to make for good will between the confessions than was any plan for drawing up a common basis of religious training." If the common sufferings under Hitler, 1933–1945, cannot secure interfaith co-operation in education between the Catholics and Protestants of Germany, what can? Those advocates of released time who hope for Catholic-Protestant understanding are doomed to disappointment.

9. *How do the public school teachers interpret the released time experiment?*

Some who formerly viewed it favorably have changed

their verdict. As far as my correspondence is concerned, not one public school teacher favored released time. Teachers feel that their task is made much more difficult and that public education itself is penalized both as to time and efficiency, and as to morale.

A very prominent western public school educator concludes his analysis thus:

In the main, the system of releasing pupils from school for this sectarian "Bible" teaching has proven a failure. Most Protestant children elect not to participate because of the poor quality of teaching. Maybe the Catholics would send more of their children to the public schools where the system obtained and thereby insure for them a quality and type of instruction definitely superior to the mediocre, provincial, and doctrinaire character of that usually obtaining in Catholic schools. It may seem necessary for the purposes of insuring adequate education for citizenship to modify our compulsory education laws so that children are in public schools at least through grade eight.

Another public school teacher writes:

The majority of pupils left in school are Protestant, and they are penalized for not going to religious instruction. Successive directives have come curtailing their activity. They may not do the things they might be permitted to do during a regular study period. They may not go to the music room, the art room, the sewing room, the typing room, the library, to a teacher for help or to make up a test. They may not stir from a 14 by 14 seat for one clock hour. *This is obviously an attempt to make school so unattractive that the pupil will elect religion rather than stay in school.*

In a recently conducted poll of representative school administrators on the topic of religious instruction in public schools, only one-third "believed" in released time for religious instruction or would personally vote to support legislation to legalize released time. One and four-tenths per cent thought the church was responsible for the training of children in religion, but 54.5 per cent placed that responsibility on the church and home.*

10. *Does the granting of credit for released time courses conflict with public school standards?*

In one of the best released time church schools, the director added this footnote to his report: "While these courses are listed by grades, they are not always offered in this order because of the necessary combination of classes in certain centers." "Grades come to the weekday church school classes as grades. Difficulty arises when some children have never had weekday or Sunday School instruction. Should work be given for the few or for the many? One teacher uses the informed to lead the others." What educational folly! Religious education began as a protest against this situation in the Sunday School and now released time has returned to it. A public school grade becomes a released time chaos. Is it any wonder that the fundamentalist chorus, "Back to our dear old Sunday School and ungraded lessons," is being chanted rather loudly again?

11. *May public education legally grant credit for released time courses?*

There is much confusion among us regarding sectarian teaching. The mere fact that several Protestant groups unite to give a course in religion does not at all make it nonsectarian so far as other Protestant groups, Jews, and Catholics are concerned. For example, Congregationalists, Baptists, and Presbyterians all use the Westminster Confession of Faith. They are Calvinists. Formerly a Calvinistic pro-

* *The Nation's Schools*, December, 1945, p. 45.

fessor of theology had often to take an oath to criticize Arminianism. For the Calvinist the Methodist was then a sectarian. Glance at the *National Catholic Almanac*, 1945. Under "Principal Heresies" are listed Anglicanism, Baptists, Calvinism, Christian Science, Congregationalism, and all the various Protestant groups down the line. In the Catholic view, a combination of three heretical groups would constitute a greater heresy.

Or consider this news item on the situation in Canada: "The general board of religious education of the Church of England in Canada, in October, 1944, warned that the home and the church must continue to feel the responsibility for religious upbringing of the children and that *the problems in religious education are not solved by religious instruction in the schools.*" This information was released by the Religious News Service, under dateline of October 27th, at Ste. Anne de Bellevue.

However, paradoxically, the board did commend the Province of Ontario for initiating regular periods of religious instruction and the plan of opening and closing school with religious moments. We presume that what the board means is that it favors the opening of the public schools every morning with a prayer, a hymn, and the reading of Scriptures, without any comments whatever on the Scriptures read.

"*Definite disapproval was expressed of the present movement to have the Bible taught in the Dominion schools by regular lay teachers.* It was the feeling of the board that Bible teachers should be persons with 'definite relationship to the Christian Church,' and the teaching of the Bible as a routine duty of the regular teachers was discussed unfavorably." But if a regular school teacher may not comment on the Bible, the Bible is really defined as a sectarian book.

When, then, does a course in religion cease to be sectarian? Evidently when it is taught as any other course in the curriculum—objectively, historically, scientifically. But if this were done, many now promoting released time would protest. If a non-churchman taught a Catholic doctrine in such a way that neither Catholic nor Lutheran nor other Protestant nor Jew nor atheist could register a valid objection, it would be non-sectarian instruction.

If the nature of the teaching in the weekday church schools is sectarian, not historical and objective, may public school credit be given for this kind of course? In the *Nation's Schools*, the answer to the question was:

> The American public school is legally nonsectarian. The granting of credit for sectarian religious instruction given by any voluntary interest groups whose educational qualifications, materials, and methods are not subject to review by the state is, first of all, of dubious legality. It is also a dangerous general institutional practice.

> If credit is given for sectarian religious instruction, the school in fact actually has given approval to the specific sectarian point of view. Since both the American state and the public schools are nonsectarian, the favoring of one sect over another is dangerous. Democracy may protect and encourage all phases of religious expression but it cannot afford to give greater aid and comfort to one than to another without endangering its entire position of impartiality.

> In the third place, it is debatable whether the school should give official credit for uncontrolled and unsupervised sectarian teaching unless it is likewise willing to give credit for unsupervised and uncontrolled commercial correspondence courses.

The sectarian nature of the teaching in weekday church schools appears from an examination of their curricula and admissions of teachers. Its propagandists claim the use of historical method and stress its interdenominational features. But in which of the courses do Catholics, Protestants, and Jews study together? Why do the Lutherans politely decline the invitation to let their members unite with other denominations to study religion? In the *same* district of a New York city, the annual report lists: "North East, Interdenominational Only, enrollment 428; Lutheran Division Only, enrollment 240."

Here are some weekday church school "historical method" questions for the seventh grade: "When you see three circles in the symbolism of the church what does it refer to?" "Give one reason for the different denominations working together *as they do* in the Federation of Churches." "Write briefly who Luther was and what he did." "The Pilgrim Fathers came to this country for what purpose?" "List several things we can do for your church." In the third grade, the center of interest is on "Learning to Know and Walk with God"; in the fourth, on "Growing into Christian Citizenship"; in the fifth, on "A Trip through the Old Testament," classifying Nehemiah among the prophets; in the sixth, on "Christ, a World Hero"; in the seventh, on "Exploring Our Church"; *the work of the Federation of Churches is presented* and a brief but appreciative look is taken into the work of the Catholic and Jewish communions"; in the eighth grade, on "Religion in School and Community"; "the first section of the course acquaints them with the importance of religion in education. It acquaints the students with the best elements in their new school environment and seeks to undergird their activities with the religious viewpoint"; in the ninth grade, on "The Teachings of Jesus"; in the tenth grade, on "The Bible—How it came to be and what it says"; *this course gives an introduction to the historical approach to the study of the Bible*"; in the eleventh grade, on "The Church through the Ages"; *it is aimed to help the pupil to build for himself as complete a philosophy of religion as is feasible at this age.*"

As far as we can discern there are many Sunday Schools with curricula as good as, and sometimes superior to, the curriculum here outlined.

When intolerance appears in a widely used Protestant parochial school textbook in such a statement as this: "The Semites were the descendants of Shem, the son of Noah who would not take an advantage of his old father. The other members of the white race, including many in northern Africa, were descendants of Japheth. But Ham, the wicked son of Noah, was the ancestor of the black race, the people who did become the servants of the white race, as God had decreed," is it to be assumed that it will be lacking in that denomination's weekday church school? But American democracy is dedicated to the ideal that "all men are created equal."

12. *What, then, is the relation between released time and American law?*

In the 1920's, church members contended that the Eighteenth Amendment must be obeyed whether one approved of it or not. It was the law. One is therefore a bit amused to read this in a weekday church school bulletin:

In view of the fact that there are diverse rulings and interpretations of the constitution and law and in the absence of any court rulings on the subject of the use of the school buildings for religious purposes, it should be known that by unanimous action or support of the entire community, such use has been authorized by local school boards in many districts in the state. *Many of these communities could never have weekday "Church Schools" unless they used the school buildings, because there is no church or other building near the district or centralized school.* However, every precaution has been taken to avoid sectarian controversy, abuse of school property, or interference with the regular school program. Districts

which use school buildings should also recognize that
more may be at stake than the question of local approval.
*To some, the use of school buildings represents a definite
violation of the state constitution, and to others it threat-
ens our time-honored principle which demands the separation of church and state.* What these problems hold for
the future growth of weekday schools is uncertain. Our
children need a more adequate religious training, but as to
whether school buildings should be used for this purpose
every local community may act in the light of its convictions about what powers are given by the law.

The opinion rendered by W. W. Potter, Attorney General of Michigan, 1928, merits republication:

1. That sectarian textbooks may not be used in the public schools;
2. That the school board has no authority to establish
   or continue courses teaching sectarian religious subjects;
3. The school board has no right to use public school
   buildings for the purpose of giving religious instruction;
4. Any textbook which stresses the doctrines of the
   Protestant church or any other church, cannot under
   the law be legally used in the public schools;
5. Public funds cannot be used by the school board to
   purchase or aid in purchasing textbooks of a religious
   or sectarian character;
6. Public funds may not be used to pay the whole or
   any part of the salary of teachers employed to give
   religious or sectarian instruction in the public schools;
7. The time of pupils in the public schools may not be
   diverted from the ordinary course of study and devoted to religious or sectarian subjects; and I may add,
8. Any member of the school board who participates in

diverting public funds to an illegal purpose may be held liable personally and on his official bond for such diversion; and

9. Inasmuch as the payment of public funds of the school district for religious instruction is prohibited, the payment of such money by the school board would constitute a misdemeanor because it would be doing an act prohibited by law, and where no other penalty is prescribed, would constitute a misdemeanor.

Here is the common-sense argument of Mr. Potter:

If the representatives of one religion or religious sect or denomination have a right to have teachers in the public schools at public expense, who take the time and attention of the pupils therein in religious instruction, then of course every other religion or religious sect or denomination must under the law, have an equal right. If Protestant teachers are employed and paid, then Catholic teachers may be employed and paid. The same rule must be applied to Jews and Gentiles, Catholics and Protestants, Theosophists, Christian Scientists, Mormons, and followers of the Israelite House of David, and to all other religious sects and denominations who desire to have their religion taught in the public schools.

13. *Is there a general religious interest in the released time experiment?*

The data in the preceding chapter show that there is considerable Catholic, Lutheran, and minor sect interest. Then the picture changes. After three decades of propaganda in behalf of the weekday church school according to the United States Religious Census, 1936, there were thirty-eight times as many pupils in Protestant Sunday Schools as in Protestant weekday church schools. Dismissed time sectarian education does not seem to be of the American way of life. Out of a total of 2,043 school systems surveyed a dozen years ago, 82 per cent had never released students for weekday religious instruction, 7.3 per cent had done so but had again discontinued the practice, 10.7 per cent were continuing so to release. Among the reasons for discontinuation of the plan were lack of funds, lack of interest, dissatisfaction with the program, lack of co-operation between the schools and the churches, the problem of occupying the time of non-dismissed children.

In 1936 there were 589,729 Roman Catholic pupils in released time schools; also 156,758 Lutherans, but only 403,-433 of all other United States religious and non-religious groups. The grand total of released time pupils amounted to less than 4 per cent of the 5 to 17 year age population.

In the hope of obtaining dependable and complete statistics for 1937 to 1945, while we wait for the United States Census of Religious Bodies for 1946, extensive correspondence was carried on with various Roman Catholic and Protestant leaders in the weekday church school movement, but without the success anticipated. Reliable general released time statistics do not seem to exist.

The hysteria, emotionalism, and reactionary tendencies which always appear during war provided every reason to assume that our total war recently ended, accompanied by increased juvenile delinquency and mass adult frustration, would enable released time propagandists tremendously to accelerate their agitation and appeal and at least double not only enrollment in released time schools after 1939 and especially after 1942 but also the number of local cells. Distressed persons in great numbers fearful of the future turned by thousands to the protection of the cults and such authoritarian types of Christianity as Fundamentalism and Roman Catholicism. For example, the number of converts to Roman Catholicism in 1928 just before the depression began came to 36,376 but in 1943, after the war was taking its toll, it rose to 90,822—an increase of 150 per cent. With the pressure reduced and victory in sight, that convert total dropped to 84,908 in 1944.

When measured against the ravages of the war years, the increase in the number of weekday church schools and their enrollment even on the claims of their leaders seems somewhat disappointing. A fair generalization is that where released time schools have been tried for years they are merely holding their own or receding. Of course new cells in quantity could be organized under contemporary pressures of social dislocations. When American psychology becomes stabilized, the weekday church school will have much more difficult going. Lately, it has begun to acclaim the values in the "necessary Sunday School."

14. *Is the released time experiment in curriculum, personnel, and leadership adequate to the religious needs of our time?*

Some think that the weekday church school might possibly be able to justify its existence if it really advanced Protestant unity, if it actually reached the non-church-going population, if it to any considerable extent reduced the religious illiteracy of the Sunday School by introducing its constituency to a historical interpretation of the Bible, if by ethicizing the content of its materials it helped promote the quest of the good life. In fact, the weekday church school the country over can hardly boast superior equipment, curricula, and personnel. There are many Sunday Schools still leading the way.

What most weekday church school enthusiasts forget is that the British government in publishing its plans for educational reconstruction in the summer of 1943 stated that "it will be open to the parent to withdraw his child from all or any form of religious worship or instruction!" The British government refused to sponsor denominational teaching in Provided Schools: "the State though concerned to ensure a sound religious basis for all education cannot take on itself the full responsibility *for fostering the teaching of formularies distinctive of particular denominations.*" If Britain with its very different tradition despairs of the task in advance, what chance of success would a parallel attempt have in the United States with its separation of church and state? Even in England, as soon as the religious question is raised, the unity of the educational process is broken down. All other subjects can be taught objectively, scientifically, with open minds. Only religion cannot risk the test of objectivity. The nearer the formal teaching of religion approaches the twentieth-century classroom, the more will the modern child conclude that such instruction is beyond understanding.

If weekday church school propagandists are not aware of how inadequate their plan is to the religious needs of the twentieth century, let them ponder this from the mind and pen of Rufus M. Jones:

Two-thirds of the entire population of the United States have no definite connection or affiliation with any form of organized Christianity. If the one-third were in every instance dedicated to Christ's way of life, the other two-thirds would soon feel the contagion of their spirit and the dynamic quality of their lives. But unfortunately a good many of those who compose the Christian third of the population are only nominal members of a church, and they reveal in their daily lives a large measure of satisfaction with, or even devotion to, what we are here calling "secular civilization." Rural centers of life which were once nurseries of religion and of high moral endeavor have undergone an ominous change. There are still rural sections in which religious interest has been cultivated and where it remains virile and vital, but there are on the other hand whole townships in all parts of America in which there is no form of organized religion and where no adequate effort is made to interpret spiritual life to the little children born within the area. . . .

Meantime the interpreters of religion yielded point after point in the bitter contest, and from time to time, drew up the lines of battle at a different battle-front, but all the time science and religion were in many essential points opposed the one to the other, and the student who accepted the conclusions of science was made to feel that he had deserted the religion of his fathers and was an enemy to the true faith. Little by little vast numbers of the student class have accepted that challenge. They have thrown in their lot and given their vote on the side of demonstration, and have allowed the cause of organized religion to shift for itself without their aid or sympathy. Almost everywhere required attendance at college chapels has come under fire, and required courses in religious teaching have become unpopular if not taboo. It is not in China alone that this situation prevails. It confronts as well many officers of those institutions of learning in the West which were founded by devoted Christians to be the centers of an uncontaminated religious culture. There is an ominous drift away from the old-time interpretations of Christianity. Where the choice is sharply drawn between declarations of faith and demonstrations of the laboratory, the students of today side with the laboratory. Where a possible hundred students will come to hear a lecture on the Christian conception of the Kingdom of God, a thousand will listen to a lecture on atoms or an interpretation of behaviorism.

A well-known professor of religious education writes:

Weekday religious education is not the answer to the quest of the church. One need not question that, in given instances, these schools have done so and so; but the total record is not impressive. And, even if it could achieve the impossible and produce a demonstration as a going concern, it would still leave the more fundamental issue of the nature of religion and the normal means of its communication from generation to generation to be answered. What boots it that the Bible has 66 books, and that the names of the Kings of Israel are so and so! Suppose you could get an agreement on the form of the Ten Commandments, so as to repeat them—how should one reach an evaluation of them in an ethical process which has not yet wholly arrived? *

15. *The most serious count in the indictment of the released time experiment is that it is deceived in regard to its own value, misinterprets the religious values found in public education, and is promoting the disintegration of public educational programs which provide the only valid general approach to religion in the American way of life.* **

Professor Emeritus Frank Otis Erb of the Colgate-Rochester Divinity School supports this interpretation when he writes:

If one is concerned that our young people shall be sent forth into the world with a keen sense of regard for personality, regard for the great freedoms, regard for the cosmic values which are the substructure of our American way, then our schools actually represent the carry-over into life of the fundamentals of all democratic religion. It is true that this is scarcely enough for church membership, but by what right do we ask the *public* school to prepare for membership in a particular church? Surely the churches themselves must prepare their youth for mem-

* Henry Burke Robins, Professor Emeritus of the Colgate-Rochester Divinity School.
** This point was the main burden of *School and Church: The American Way* (New York: Harper and Brothers, 1944). To appreciate the thesis, that volume should be studied.

bership in a particular church. It is an unwarranted and a dangerous demand, dangerous both to church and school, that our schools shall forsake their public character in order to relieve the churches of what they should regard as their own sacred duty and privilege.

It was a teacher in the Syracuse, New York, schools who addressed the Editor of *The Post Standard* thus:

Last Sunday many thousands listened to some of our leading citizens discuss future plans for our schools over the air in "Syracuse on Trial." Our superintendent of Syracuse schools told us, in the few minutes assigned to him, of the expansion of school services we may need to make after the war, or even sooner.

I wish he could have talked about our usual program, some of the things we are doing now. This would be of great interest to those who are parents, and to all taxpayers. For instance there is the matter of religious education, which came up briefly at the end of the discussion, and about which we are all profoundly concerned. There is so much that could be said other than that some children go once weekly on school time for religious instruction.

The children in our public schools are having daily experience in religious education. The search for the truth as experienced in all their learning, excellence in performance of a task, reverence for that which is beautiful and good, respect for every other person, fairness and justice in dealings with others, and, the crowning glory of true religion, the kindness which surpasses justice, all are religious experiences. And perhaps the experience of living and working together with children, and grown-ups, of all faiths and national backgrounds is one way in which we come closest to the actual teachings of Jesus.

We who are engaged in school work know better than

anyone else wherein we fall short of these ideals. But the fact remains they are the ideals of the free and democratic public school system of America, whose establishment was one of the greatest steps ever taken toward the achievement of democracy and the application of Christian principles.

We do not teach doctrines or dogma, nor attempt to interpret theology. These are the responsibility of the children's homes and the church of the parents' choice. To do so in school would be to favor one faith and deny many, and therefore undemocratic. But true religion we do teach daily, Syracuse parents, as we try to lead your children in the ways of truth, responsibility, and Christian kindness.

The author of *Our National Enemy Number One, Education without Religion* may have missed this.

When the released time program is articulated with the new religious synthesis developing in modern life, it may have a part to play in constructing the American way. Millions of Americans have now accepted that synthesis. In a practical sense most Americans use it without abandoning the inherited religious contradictions. The final section of this study will consider its main elements. Point 15, therefore, awaits its complete apology in chapters XI to XV.

Part Three

*The Emergence of a New Synthesis
Based upon the Scientific Spirit
and the Democratic Faith*

Chapter Eleven

Understanding American Education

The path of American education has led away from ecclesiastical and sectarian control toward the scientific spirit and the democratic faith. It represents free inquiry. It cannot be shackled by a Vatican directive or frightened by a Protestant threat. A proof text from the Bible would merely be critically analyzed. It respects facts. It tries properly to interpret the American environment and to fit the student to play his part well in the drama of life. Adjustment to individual and social needs is not feared and social creativeness is highly valued.

Public education has become the most significant American institution because the democratic way of life demands a higher educational level than any other form of government. It is for all the people but does not compel conformity. Private and parochial schools may coexist with it. But the wealth of all the citizens must share the cost of education free and open to all the children of the nation. Public education is not a charity. In its opposition to the current attempt to give federal funds to the parochial schools, the Greater Detroit and Wayne County CIO Council formulated the American point of view thus: "The public education highway is the public school system, and if that is not good enough for you, it is your privilege to build your own private education highway, but why should public funds be given to those who despise and ignore the public school system?" The point has never been made more aptly. Public education recognizes the people's will as sovereign. Its creed is progress by evolution, not by revolutions which produce ruins. It emphasizes both knowledge and wisdom and through their integration develops within each of its students greater competency to interpret life. In an age insisting upon publicity it goes quietly about its task and therefore is occasionally criticized when it should be complimented. It "fosters the growth of the individual in his setting." It prefers "a head full of ideas to a head full of facts." Its aim is to enable the American youth to live more successfully in the one-world environment which is at its dawn by impressing upon him the unity, continuity, and developmental nature of life. All life is interrelated. The present comes out of the past and conditions the future. Progress is conditioned by structure.

In the report entitled "Desirable Social-Economic Goals of America" heredity and strength, physical security, participation in an evolving culture, an active flexible personality, a suitable occupation, economic security, mental security, equality of opportunity, freedom, and fair play were stressed as objectives toward which education must lead the way. Thus American education is for life, not death.

The seven fundamental human needs which are the particular concern of public education are health, command of the fundamental processes, worthy home membership, economic adjustment, worthy citizenship, the worthy use of leisure time, and ethical character. "The true test of civilization is not the census nor the size of cities nor the crops—no, but the kind of man the country turns out."

Contemporary American education teaches the child worthy individual and social ideals, cultivates in him the power of self-direction, self-appraisal, self-control, and the desire and ability to work co-operatively with others.

Public education may not foster sectarianism, for, "with sectarian teaching there is no whole course of religious study, only a restricted sectarian course, and there is therefore no free play of children's abilities. The sectarian aim is to keep the antagonisms between the creeds alive, not to dissolve them; to ensure that the sects retain their identities; to perpetuate their distinctive alignments and make their divergencies as pronounced in post-school social life. There is no training for citizenship. It fosters neither good will nor a sense of the brotherhood of man. . . ."

If the religions of the world could be studied educationally, historically, objectively, scientifically, unemotionally, the American educational curriculum might offer formal courses in religion. But then the student would hear about "the birth of religious worship with the belief that everything is inhabited by a migrant spirit," about "mana," about the worship of divine priests and kings, about families of gods, about Shintoism, Taoism, Confucianism, Buddhism, Hinduism, Judaism, Humanism. The student might read Frazer's *Golden Bough* or the *Sacred Books of the East* or Frazer's *Folklore in the Old Testament*. Indeed, he might discover the *Apocrypha* or the *Pseudepigrapha*. The historical method of studying the Bible would send the student to his religious counselor with many perplexing questions. The ministers might soon be objecting "that if instruction in Christianity is linked with instruction in other religions, children will come to regard all faiths as equally interesting, false, and worthless. That sounds like a cry of despair voiced by people who have little confidence in the efficacy of their labors."

In a lesson in history, a competent teacher would discuss and compare sources, mention divergent opinions and the evidence pro and con, advance tentative hypotheses, encourage intelligent questions and answers from students. "But in his divinity lessons," says Gotch, the student "finds that he is required to accept without comment or criticism, statements of alleged fact, many of which he naturally considers as insults to his reason; any attempt to exercise his critical faculty is discouraged and his questions are for the most part ignored or evaded. His intellect remains unsatisfied; gradually his antagonism is aroused, and finally interest fades into indifference. In his opinion 'Divinity' has been tried and found wanting."

American education has won its long battle against sectarianism. The sects themselves will help keep it won. Nevertheless the one world of the United Nations' Charter may indirectly introduce millions of Americans to the history of religions with devastating consequences for orthodoxy. For the student may ask whether American Christianity is Christian and how many American Christian customs are of pagan origin. Charles Smith dealing with this problem in *The Teacher's Case for Religious Instruction* says:

. . . Many of the customs in the English tradition are indubitably of heathen origin. Evidences of this are to be seen in several directions: in the names of the days of the week, the seasons, and the stormy elements; in certain taboos, magic emblems, and mascots, and in totemic heraldry; in the interest in fairies, demons, witches, and diviners; in such festivals as Yule, Easter, May Day, Midsummer Eve, and Hallowe'en; in relics of tree worship and the veneration of Nature's shrines; in dedicatory rites like those accompanying the launching of ships and the laying of foundation stones; in the popular attitude towards war and the exaltation of valorous deeds; in the existence of an official and regular priesthood attendant upon the Court and State; in funeral, marriage, coronation, and various initiation ceremonies; and in the prevalent notions of survival after death, of re-incarnations, of the spirit world, of the higher world—Isles of the Blest and Valhalla, and of the lower world—the Abyss and Hell. These are a few evidences of the persistence of Celtic and Teutonic religious cults which play a larger part in people's affections than is commonly supposed or acknowledged.

When a college student is introduced to Durkheim's theory of religion, he reports a big headache over the week end. He must be told that the totem is not the object of worship but merely a symbol of something which is adored. That something is the social group, the clan, the sib. Hence the clan worships itself, that is, the real god of the clan is the clan. Society protects and preserves and disciplines the individual and therefore is god. The goal of religion is the integration of society rather than the adjustment of the individual to an unseen power. Religion is then no longer an illusion but a reality because it is based upon an actual social subdivision known as sib. Now, hearing all this for the first time and confronting his counselor with "collectivism" and receiving no satisfactory explanation, the student is still "dizzy" when the subject is continued in the Monday class period.

But, if such a simple theory of the origin of religion perplexes the student trained in authoritarian religion, what will occur when the deficiencies of his own "given" faith are brought to his attention? Whether the problems of religion are approached historically, sociologically, philosophically, or psychologically in a modern college classroom, similar disasters result. In the American context there can be only archaeological interest in the nails of the cross, the sponge, the robe, the winding sheet, the stone which killed Stephen, the pants of Thomas of Canterbury, *Abraxas*, *Abracadabra*, and churchyard earth good for tuberculosis. In self-defense the churches will shortly be compelled to set up historical curricula in their Sunday Schools. Inherited dogmas—those dead hands of the past preventing growth—made by men to meet existing emergencies at rough and tumble religious assemblies and not at all revealed from Heaven, can no longer be cited as final. When "national planning in industry, business, agriculture and government, expansion of insurance systems to cover protection against sickness, old age, unemployment, universal education from earlier years to adult education, the perfection of systems of transportation, the development of city, community, regional and state planning, the development of national, state and local parks, preventive medicine, deliberate encouragement of science, letters and the arts, the preservation and expansion of a reasoned equality of opportunity for all men and women to unfold their talents and co-operation in internationalism and peace"—to employ Mr. Beard's enumeration—are the items of contemporary public interest, can the churches hope to retain Johnny's attention when discussing the names of the twelve apostles or what Thomas Aquinas said?

"Appreciation of health, love of beauty, enjoyment of intellectual discovery, devotion to freedom and democracy, interest in play and recreation, social uses of wealth and invention, the enrichment of social fellowship and the spirit of altruism permeating all relationships" are according to Harold Saxe Tuttle the aims of our schools. How then can a released time course concentrating on whether Jesus immediately after his baptism started his preaching and healing ministry, withdrew to the wilderness for meditation, or started on a journey to Jerusalem figure in Susan's experience? What child cares about the ignorance of Jesus' disciples or whether the earliest gospel was written by Mark, Matthew, or John? Of far greater concern to any American child is the understanding of life, self, what life offers, and how progress comes. He lives in the American democracy, not in the times of the Councils of Nicaea and Chalcedon.

The American child as time goes on will discover more and more that education is "adjustment between people and their surroundings." Education's conflict with religion is becoming anachronistic in the presence of the problems being created by the machine. To quote from a friend's unpublished manuscript:

We need to show more intelligence in the further development of our system of education, which conditions our use of Power Age tools and techniques and which should stimulate the conquest of more freedom for the individual and the achievement of a better balance in our way of living. . . . We live in the midst of a conflict which may lead to another Dark Age in human development or to a Golden Age surpassing any incline ever ascended by human beings in their conquest of freedom. The central problem seems to be that of *cultural lag*, or the tendency for human beings to fall behind in making some adaptations between themselves and their surroundings while other adaptations or activities speed up. Education can operate to increase or decrease the amount of cultural lag. . . . Beneath a thin veneer of kindliness and wisdom won through our long and painful strivings toward human freedom lies the Neanderthal brute controlled by hunger, pain, fear, and rage. He breaks forth periodically in such cruel and fantastic forms as feudalism, imperialism, militarism, Fascism, and rockets. . . . Scientific invention and the control of our physical surroundings have tremendously speeded up. . . . In one way the overemphasis on power, speed, and scientific invention is forcing us to realize the need for social invention or human engineering. It can help us to bridge the Grand Canyon which has grown up between people who are concerned with social relationships, such as teachers, politicians, merchants, and farmers; and people who are techniciaᵤs, expert in the control of our natural surroundings, such as physicists, engineers, navigators, and chemists.*

It would seem to be the duty of religious education even at this late hour to abandon its archaeological interest and make some contribution to the solution of the problem of cultural lag by overcoming to a slight extent at least its own religious lag. Let it "devote its full energy to social invention, or human engineering" and do something about the problems created by human inertia in the religious area.

Is this too dangerous a quest in the presence of the inevitable religious reaction? The National Council of Congregational Churches of the United States was not so timid in 1925 when it observed that the translation of the ethical ideal of Jesus into education means:

(1) The building of a social order in which every child has the best opportunity for development. (2) Adequate and equal educational opportunity for all, with the possibility of extended training for those competent. (3) A thorough and scientific program of religious and secular education designed to Christianize everyday life and conduct. (4) Conservation of health, including careful instruction in sex hygiene and home building, abundant and wholesome recreation facilities, and education for leisure, including a nation-wide system of adult education. (5) Insistence on constitutional rights and duties, including freedom of speech, of the press, and of peaceable assemblage. (6) Constructive education and Christian care of dependents, defectives, and delinquents, in order to restore them to normal life whenever possible, with kindly segregation for those who are hopelessly feeble-minded. (This means that such institutions as the jails,

* See *School and Society*, Jan. 26, 1946, article "Toward a New History of Education," by Arthur H. Moehlman.

prisons, and orphan asylums should be so conducted as to be genuine centers for education and health.) (7) A scientifically planned program of international education promoting peace and good will and exposing the evils of war, intoxicants, illiteracy, and other social sins.

For years Chave has been urging that spiritual goals are being realized when "the sense of worth, social sensitivity, appreciation of the universe, discrimination in values, responsibility and accountability, co-operative fellowship, quest for truth and realization of ideals, integration of experience, language and symbols for adequate expression of ideas and ideals, that is, growing ability to express the highest values and ambitions, and the observance of special times and ceremonies for keeping sensitive to higher values" are in the curriculum of religious education.

To be sure, this is not catechism but it is the path that must now be taken by any vital American religious education. For, Chave continues, sense of worth signifies the "awakening of qualities superior to blind animal behavior or regimented mechanical responses"; social sensitivity, "learning to understand and appreciate persons who are different"; appreciation of the universe, "the discovery that the processes of the universe are such that personal and social values may be furthered when right adjustments are made"; discrimination in values, "the recognition of lower and higher values in all phases of life and the readiness to sacrifice lower for larger or higher gains"; responsibility and accountability, "a growing sense of the right use of freedom and the recognition that no one can be a law unto himself but is accountable to the others on whom he depends"; co-operative fellowship, "a sense of the privileges in belonging to a good home, neighborhood, community, or other social unit"; quest for truth and realization of ideals, "the recognition that spiritual insight and achievement of better ways of living are normal processes of growth when one seeks the highest"; integration of experience, "the growing ability to meet success or failure, achievement or frustration with poise, a balanced sense of the values and significant goals for living"; language and symbols, "the finding of ways to share experiences and the utilization of the fine arts, poetry, and drama to express spiritual meanings and values"; special celebrations, "keeping the focus of attention on the high values and goals which history has proved vital to individual and collective living."

Only when the study of the Bible is humanized can it again become meaningful to the average American child. Only when religious education sheds the grave clothes in which authoritarianism has buried it may it hope to rise from the tomb of preserving a past that is gone to an ethical interpretation of American life as it is. A desperate world is pleading with it to bridge the gap between the soulless machine and its devastating possibilities and the creation of "an harmonious balance between ourselves and our surroundings." American youth cannot return to the simple life of the founding fathers. It must live in the presence of airplane, sound films, mass production, greater and better bombs, and one world. It seeks new religious values in a world "strewn with the wreckage of civilizations which could not maintain a balance between people and their surroundings." American education will help youth discover them. If religious education needs an authoritarian warrant to reconstruct its curriculum, it might find it in that admonition of the long ago: "Let the dead bury the dead, follow thou me."

Chapter Twelve

Understanding the Christian Heritage

Contemporary Christianity is heavily burdened by the
dead weight of the past. Its doctrine of "apostolic succession" is a myth. Its identification of the church with the
"true Israel" paved the way for the faith in its pre-existence.
It has contradictory interpretations of the sacraments which
confuse the laity. Its Christology is post-New Testament,
although the New Testament itself presents Jesus as the son
of Joseph and Mary in its earliest strata and as a wonder-
child only in the later layers of two late gospels. Jesus himself raised the question as to how the Messiah could be of
David's line. His immediate family, Mark says, regarded
Jesus as out of his mind. He taught that only God is good
and did not know when the world would end. His life was
a personal achievement, and he had need of prayer. The
church at Jerusalem called him Messiah but associated
messianity only with suffering, death, exaltation, and sway,
never relating his death to the forgiveness of sins. Acts
8:32,33 quotes the wrong verses from Isaiah in behalf of
the new view of the death of Jesus. It was Paul who interpreted Jesus as pre-existent Son of God and yet Paul
never resorted to a virgin birth view or let Jesus become
truly human. His nature only resembled man's sinful nature.
Only in Matthew 1:18ff. and Luke 1:26ff. did Jesus become

141

a wonder-child as to his birth and in Matthew 27:51ff. and John 20:1ff. as to his death. In the Johannine literature Jesus finally became God and Savior. The earliest sonship of Jesus was appointive, ethical, beginning at the resurrection or at his baptism by John. The later sonship of Jesus was metaphysical, pre-existent. Within a few decades the man of Nazareth became in Christian faith the creator of the cosmos and later God and Savior.

The legend of the Jerusalem and apostolic origin of the Apostles' Creed dates from the fourth century. Actually there was an Eastern Apostles' Creed, an early Roman Apostles' Creed, a later Roman Creed. Then the Apostles' Creed disappeared at Rome because the heretical Goths could not repeat it. It migrated to Gaul and when it re-appeared in Rome in the eighth century it had been enlarged by the addition of "maker of heaven and earth," "conceived by," "suffered," "dead," "He descended into hell," "God," "Almighty," "Catholic," "communion of saints," and "life everlasting." There are at least ten different views concerning Christ's descent to the realm of the dead. And J. Rendel Harris has solved the problem of I Peter 3:19 by letting Enoch preach to the imprisoned spirits.* As to "the communion of the saints" there is no agreement regarding its meaning. In A.D. 1543 "of the body" was substituted for "of the flesh" in the eleventh affirmation.

To summarize the controversies over the Nicene Creed and the Creed of Chalcedon would require too much space. But this endless doctrinal wrangling caused the Monophysites to welcome the Arabs as saviors, and today Mohammedanism classifies the culture of the Greek church of southern Russia as paganism.

Historical study has shown that creeds are formulas, arising out of definite religious situations, designed to meet urgent present needs, and serving as tests of orthodoxy.

* See footnote in Moffatt's translation, *The Holy Bible.*

They have not been able to secure uniformity of belief and have never anticipated the problems which would face the churches of the future. The Apostles' Creed gives no information regarding the attitude Christianity should take on disarmament, internationalism, race prejudice, woman's rights, the Charter of the United Nations. The creeds make religion an intellectual affair and result in the mischievous "symbolical" interpretation of Christianity.

For some decades to come, Christian education will be based on the Bible. But this Bible is not the Bible of the historian but that of tradition with its unhistorical claims of verbal inspiration. No writer of either the Old Testament or the New Testament expected his composition to be included in a sacred list of books binding upon faith and practice. No writer of the Old Testament claimed anything for the totality of writings now included in it. How could he? The canon of the Old Testament was not finally closed until the second century of the Christian era. Every reference to inspiration in the New Testament involving a collection of books applies to the Old Testament. For the early Christians the Jewish Bible was inspired, and there was no New Testament in existence. It was A.D. 200 before the New Testament in shorter form existed, and the fourth century before the canonicity of the present collection of twenty-seven books was settled. The Bible of Jesus and of Paul was the Jewish holy book. Neither assumed that there would ever be another Bible. Indeed, it has often been asserted that "Jesus was not a Christian but a Jew" and that Paul was "the first Christian." Yet Paul's writings are saturated with more than fourscore direct quotes from the Old Testament. The first generation of Christians possessed only one Bible, namely, the volume today called the Old Testament.

The Old Testament is part and parcel of western civilization. Its abandonment would entail irreparable losses in literature, music, painting, architecture, drama, religion, ethics, and government.

Nietzsche knew this:

> In the Jewish Old Testament, the book of divine justice, there are men, occurrences, speeches in so great a style for which the Greek and Indian writings provide nothing comparable. One stands in astonishment and awe before these grand survivals of what man once was. When Asia's little peninsula called Europe sets itself up in contrast with Asia as "progress of mankind" one's thoughts are sad enough. . . . Taste for the Old Testament is a test of "small" and "great". . . .

Friedrich Delitzsch knew this:

> Neither in Indian, Babylonian nor Semitic poetry is to be found a collection of songs which in their poetic beauty and above all in the immersion of the self in the riddle of human life, as well as in the expression of the purest religious feeling, can even approximately compare with the Old Testament Psalms. They pass from the softest notes to triumphant paean in their hymn of confidence in God. Indeed, they stand alone in the literature of the world.

That great Biblical scholar, J. M. P. Smith, of the University of Chicago, knew this:

> Great literature is that in which the splendor of great ideas is matched by the splendor of the language in which they are clothed. It is this perfect union that makes the Old Testament supremely great as literature. The New Testament here must cede the palm of preeminence to the old. While on the whole superior in the high quality of its spiritual and ethical ideals, the New Testament was not written by men possessed of a discriminating taste for

words and a fine sense of form. But in the Old Testament we find historical narrative, imaginative story, prophetic oratory, gnomic philosophy, lyric poetry, and dramatic argument at their very best. If this proposition needs further support than my poor judgment affords, let me cite the opinions of those who have a better right to speak upon literary matters than I. Tennyson, for example, pronounced the Book of Job "the greatest poem whether of ancient or modern times," Carlyle in his *Lectures on Heroes* said of the same poem, "I call it apart from all theories as if it were not Hebrew. Such a noble universality, different from noble patriotism or noble sectarianism, reigns in it. A noble Book; all men's Book. . . . There is nothing written, I think, in the Bible or out of it, of equal literary merit." Addison declares that Horace and Pindar when compared with the Hebrew Psalter display "an absurdity and confusion of style" and "a comparative poverty of imagination." I need not weary you with further citations of similar judgments, of which there is no lack. I will only say that the minister who wishes to become master of the grand style can do no better than to soak his mind in the apt phraseology and glowing imagery of the Old Testament.

Yet, if the Old Testament is to play a part in the world of the future, it must be historically understood. Because the Catholicism of Germany did not appreciate this, it suffered defeat by the Nazis who did.

The apology of the Catholic Church in Germany for the Old Testament when finally formulated came to this: The Catholic Church has ever taught that the Old Testament was given by God. The abandonment of the Old Testament signifies the destruction of the authority of the Catholic Church. The rejection of the Old Testament is the rejection of Jesus whose person, teachings, and life are inseparably interwoven with the Old Testament. Moreover, the Old Testament became a Christian book by allegorization and symbolism. The God of the Old Testament is the God of the New Testament and the Christian trinity. Although the God of the Old Testament is just and terrible, He is also loving, merciful, and kind. The God of the New Testament is Judge as well as Father. The God of the Bible is one, and intolerant only of other gods. God has always been universal, never tribal, never national. The Bible was intended to be a religious book availing itself of pictorial rather than scientific methods of expression. Hope of immortality pervades the Old Testament from beginning to end. The Psalter was the Prayer Book of Jesus and is of the Church.

For all these and other reasons, argued the Catholicism of Germany, the Old Testament must to the end of the age remain an essential part of the Christian Bible. But the Nazis satirized, ridiculed, and repudiated this Catholic defense of the Old Testament, showing that the theory of verbal inspiration arose in post-Biblical times and that the development of monotheism from faith in a tribal god, Yahweh, is held by both Catholic and Protestant scholars and that the admission of allegorization to make the Old Testament a Christian book is fatal to the entire Catholic argument. Hence, Nazism abolished the Old Testament. The only defense of the Old Testament today is the use of historical method.

In his *An Introduction to the History of History*, Shotwell describes what occurred with respect to the composition, canonization and Christianization of the Old Testament under the guise of an Hellenic Bible:

> *Suppose that the heritage of Hellas had been preserved to us in the form of a Bible. What would be the character of the book?* We should begin, perhaps, with

a few passages from Hesiod on the birth of the gods and the dawn of civilization mingled with fragments of the *Iliad* and both set into long excerpts from Herodotus. The dialogues of Plato might be given by Homeric heroes and the text of the great dramatists (instead of the prophets) be preserved interspersed one with another and clogged with the uninspired and uninspiring comments of Alexandrian savants. Imagine that the sense of their authority was so much obscured as centuries passed, that philosophers—for philosophers were to Greece what the theologians were to Israel—came to believe that *the large part of this composite work of history and philosophy had been first written down by Solon as the deliverance of the oracle of Apollo at Delphi.* Then, finally, imagine that the text became stereotyped and sacred, even the words taboo, and became the heritage of alien peoples who knew nothing more of Greek history than what this compilation contained. Such, with some little exaggeration, would be a *Hellenic Bible* after the fashion of the Bible of the Jews.

By reversing this process and getting back to the origin of the documents of the Old Testament, the dreaded historical method reveals just how Genesis 1:1 became the first verse in the Jewish Bible. And Christianity ought no longer to restrict the telling of this story to students in theological seminaries who must promptly forget it to survive in their pastorates. This esoteric knowledge must become common knowledge or the ministers will be unable to use the verses of the Old Testament even as points of departure for their sermons.

Martin Luther on the title page of his New Testament published at Wittenberg in September, 1522, enumerated only twenty-three of its twenty-seven books. He separated Hebrews, James, Jude, and the Revelation of John from his twenty-three favorites. In the titles of these "saint" appears;

in the titles of the four, it is omitted. He leaves a space between his main list and his secondary list. He lifts Hebrews
and James out of their regular order after Philemon. For
him the epistles of Paul and Peter were far superior to the
synoptic gospels. His primary New Testament consisted of
the Gospel and First Epistle of John, some of Paul's letters,
and I Peter. He repudiated I John 5:7, the verse about the
Three Heavenly Witnesses composed by a heretic of the
fourth century. His secondary New Testament consisted of
the synoptic gospels, Acts, the rest of the Pauline correspondence, II Peter, II and III John. His third New Testament contained James, Hebrews, Jude, and the Revelation
of John. For him the Bible as such was not the word of
God *but only contained it*. He decided whether a verse was
"right." The Epistle of James was not apostolic, only a
"right strawy epistle." Jude was copied from II Peter.
The Revelation of John he did not consider as either
prophetic or apostolic. Acts 7:4 was severely criticized. The
allegory of Sarah and Hagar of Galatians 4 was "too weak
to hold." James 2:24 was declared "not true" and James 1:6
as the "only and best place in the entire epistle." The Augsburg Confession contains no article upon the Bible and no
list of canonical books. Holtzmann has observed that "all
Lutheran orthodox witnesses, 1517 to 1618, deny seven
books canonical authority."

The descent from this original Protestant free attitude
toward the Bible to the later enslavement under literalism
and verbal inspiration was rapid. The Apocrypha were declared to be human writings. The sixty-six books of the
Protestant Bible in their original Hebrew and Greek form
were treated as "immediately inspired by God, *and by his
singular care and providence kept pure in all ages*"! And yet,
the Samaritan Pentateuch has some 6,000 variants from the
Massoretic text. Jerome wrote: "For if we are to pin our
faith to the Latin texts, it is for our opponents to tell us

which; since there are almost as many forms of texts as there are copies." In 1590, a Vulgate text was issued which was affirmed to be "true, legitimate, authentic, and indubitable," but two years later another text differing in thousands of instances was substituted for this "authentic" text. The eighth edition of Tischendorf varies from the seventh edition by more than 3,500 instances. It was said of John Mill, the master textual critic of England of Bentley's time, that his New Testament noted 30,000 variations in the manuscripts of the New Testament. From the *textus receptus* the manuscript Sinaiticus differs in 3,392 instances. No two of the over 4,000 Greek papyri, uncials, cursives, lectionaries employed for the construction of the text of the New Testament are now in perfect agreement. The Swiss Formula Consensus, 1675, maintained the divine inspiration of the Hebrew vowel points, although no text of the time of Jesus or several centuries thereafter contained vowel points. It thus conferred plenary inspiration upon post-Christian Hebrew scholars without ever noticing how humorous the consequences would be! But, if the Hebrew text of the Old Testament in the time of Jesus and Paul was not thus fixed, the doctrine of verbal inspiration committed harakiri. It would have been much more profitable for the brethren to have discovered the strata in both Old Testament and New Testament. Historically approached, the Old Testament becomes a chief sourcebook in religion, and the New Testament becomes selected reminiscences of the career of Jesus, some early Christian correspondence, notes upon the story of emerging Christianity, and that Utopian analysis of the primitive Christian environment called The Revelation.

The Bible is a monument to religious experience, a history of the growth of the Hebrew-Christian religion, and this relativity of the Bible is not a cause for alarm. No one despises the religious experience of an Amos, a Hosea, an

Isaiah, a John. One is interested in all past interpretations of religion as value judgments. But he insists also upon his own experience as important. If it contradicts what has gone before, he may re-examine it but cannot deny it if true. If the Bible were to be studied in such a way as to ascertain its worth for the religious and ethical life of today, it might become more than a best seller. It might again help shape man's quest after the higher values of life. As Goethe concluded: "As all our wanderings in the East were occasioned by the Sacred Scriptures, so, finally, we came back to them as to the most refreshing sources which, although sometimes muddy, spring pure and fresh from the hidden earth."

Why should not everybody know about the four decalogues of the Old Testament found in Exodus 23 and 34 and Deuteronomy 5 and Exodus 20 and their Egyptian, Babylonian, and Buddhist parallels and the romantic story of the evolution of their meaning? Has not each commandment in the traditional decalogue lost its original meaning? Does not the Hebrew enumeration of the ten commandments differ from that of the Greek Church, the Reformed churches, and the Anglican Church on the one hand, and from the Roman Catholic Church and the Lutheran Church on the other? Were not the eighth and the tenth commandments the reasons in part for Puritanism's aid to nascent capitalism? Has not the tenth commandment been the bulwark of the *status quo?* Has not contemporary America placed the Sabbath commandment in tenth place?

Why should not the true story of the Lord's Prayer be taught in religious education? It exists in various forms in the New Testament. Its doxology was added by the *Didache.* It contains Hebrew forms which even today any Jew can recite. Jesus here joins with his disciples in a prayer for the forgiveness of sins: "Forgive *us our* debts." "And lead us not into temptation" is a "hard petition." The Lord's

Prayer contains the *Gospel of Jesus* which is not the gospel of Romans 3:21–26. And thus we come to the main contradiction regarding the Lord's Prayer. It is recited regularly in the worship services of the Christian churches without the discovery on the part of the worshiping throngs that it is a statement of the *Gospel of Jesus,* affirming the Fatherhood of God and ethical forgiveness! How can the prayer be recited in the presence of theologies denying it? Father, we desire the better community, trust Thee for daily food and, because we have forgiven others, hope for forgiveness from Thee. We know that Thou wilt sustain us in all life's experiences. That is all. *It is the prayer of humanity.* There is no specifically Christian emphasis in it. All men of good will desire these things. Until this prayer is removed from the worship of the Christian churches there is a ray of hope that their theologies may yet be ethicized.

When, instead of employing historical method, the interpreter of the Bible applies passages like Colossians 3:22 and 4:1, originally concerned with ancient master-slave relations, to twentieth-century employer-employee relations, only ethical confusion results.

If the modern churches could adopt a historical attitude toward the Christian heritage, admit the findings regarding creeds, sacraments, apostolic succession, the cross, the Bible, the crusades, Christendom, they might much more readily work together to lead the present age into world reconstruction.

Chapter Thirteen

Understanding the Contemporary Social Order

There has been endless argument regarding Christendom's contribution to progress. Did it retard or accelerate the growth of modern ideas? Within Christendom there have always been minorities favoring the application of Judaeo-Christian ethical principles to existing conditions. Yet the trend of Christendom itself has been somewhat reactionary. At least while the church held sway, departures from what was were frowned upon. The most recent solution of the controversy has been proposed by Maritain. He holds that the achievements of the modern age are not the direct result of the church's presence in it but the indirect deposit of the gospel. During Christendom's period of sway, this gospel went underground and remained concealed *until the secular conscience compelled it to ascend to full view.* Is one to conclude, then, that "evangelical inspiration" and the progress of Christendom were antithetical? If faith in progress, in the infinite worth of the human personality and of all peoples, in the sovereignty of the people from whom the authority of the ruler derives, in justice and law, in liberty, fraternity, and equality grew on strange underground plants during the period of Christendom's golden age, nourished by the fertilizing power of the inspiration of the original gospel, and could come to blossom only in the secularized modern age—what strange plants, strange soil, strange climate! If the modern secular conscience is the original gospel in action, would not secularization seem to be most desirable even from the Christian point of view? "Evangelical inspiration" is an axiom of faith, not always a fact of history.

Take, for example, woman's slow ascent to something like equality with man in the secular contemporary world. Did Christendom oppose or promote that rise to equality?

In his autobiography Professor George H. Palmer comments that "Jesus frankly treated Fatherhood anthropomorphically. This fact should be borne in mind when we read the two ascetic passages in which the father's act is treated as pollution and a long train of disasters is launched on the modern world. There is no evidence that this attack on the family called the Virgin Birth was known to Jesus himself, to his mother, his disciples or to Paul." For the first generation of Christians the birth process was not sinful, and there were no theological consequences for the offspring. Original sin and guilt were unknown. No virgin birth was necessary to prevent pollution by the father, no immaculate conception to prevent pollution by the mother, no baptism to cancel the effects of original sin, no "churching of women" to atone for motherhood. Her sex did not discount a woman. In Christianity, "there was neither male nor female."

Time marched on. Somebody in the second century wrote: "Let a woman learn in silence with all submission. For I do not allow a woman to teach, or to exercise authority over men; but she is to keep quiet. For Adam was formed first, then Eve. *And Adam was not deceived, but the woman was deceived and was in sin.* Yet women will be saved by child-bearing, if they continue in faith and love and holiness and modesty" (I Timothy 2:11–15). This male estimate of woman fixed her status in Christendom. Woman was inferior, responsible for sin (and original sin somewhat later), and could be saved only by becoming a mother. Tertullian, so orthodox he joined the Montanists, called women "the devil's gateway, the unsealer of that forbidden tree. You are the first deserter of the divine law. You are she who persuaded Adam when the devil was not valiant enough to attack. You destroyed so easily God's image." Woman became a human being of secondary rank and marriage was made inferior to virginity and superior only to promiscuity. For bearing a child a mother had to be churched, readmitted to the church—a rite now elevated to "thanksgiving after childbirth." The sixteenth-century Prayer Book entitles the ceremony: "An order for the purification of women after childbirth." Before the door of the church, the woman said: "Thou shalt purge me, O Lord, with hyssop." At least as early as the fourth century, women who had given birth to a son were excluded for eighty days from attendance upon church. Prior to being duly churched, a young mother was not to be visited or to visit. In the sixth century and again in the sixteenth, churchmen debated whether or not woman was human. When woman was made a witch, the nadir of her ecclesiastical degradation was reached. Monasticism and celibacy were Christendom's condemnation of sex.

In mid-nineteenth century the woman's rights movement was born. In 1840, the World Antislavery Convention met in London. Some American women delegates were excluded and naturally inferred that the "cause of emancipation affected them as well as the slaves." Meeting at Seneca Falls, July 19, 1848, American women wrote a declaration of sentiments and resolutions, containing:

All men *and women* are created equal. The history of mankind is a history of repeated injuries and usurpations on the part of man toward woman, having in direct object the establishment of an absolute tyranny over her.

He has made her, if married, in the eye of the law, civilly dead.

In the covenant of marriage, she is compelled to promise obedience to her husband, he becoming, to all intents
and purposes, her master—the law giving him power to
deprive her of her liberty, and to administer chastisement.

He allows her in Church . . . but a subordinate position, *claiming Apostolic authority for her exclusion from
the ministry and, with some exceptions, from any public
participation in the affairs of the Church. . . .*

Resolved, that woman has too long rested satisfied in
the circumscribed limits which corrupt customs and a
perverted application of the Scriptures have worked out
for her. . . .

Similarly, planned parenthood is opposed by some
churches and is only gradually securing the mild approval
of other churches. Approbation has been expressed by such
bodies as British and American Anglicanism, the Federal
Council of Churches and the Central Conference of American Rabbis. But surely the health of mother and child,
happiness in married life, relief of overpopulation, improvement of race, prevention of poverty, and progress of civilization are ethical. Indeed not only in the rhythm system but
also in the encyclical on marriage of Pius XI, 1930, with its
paragraph summarized as "the Church also knows well that
in certain cases 'one of the parties is sinned against rather
than sinning' and the Church also declares that it is not
against nature if the marriage act is done 'in the proper
manner' but under circumstances—'either of time or of
certain defects'—that make conception impossible," ap-
peasement of birth control seems present. And Catholic
parents seek the necessary information at clinics providing
instruction in planned parenthood. Eugenics is conscious,
intelligent organic evolution.

The churches have worked in behalf of peace and internationalism, but the Italian conquest of Ethiopia was de-

fined as a "just war" and called a "Catholic crusade."
Franco was backed because the dictator was "defending the
Church in Spain." The Rhine League and the Hanseatic
League did quite as much for peace in the thirteenth century
as Christendom. Kant published *Zum Ewigen Frieden* in
1795. It was Nietzsche who wrote:

> Perhaps a memorable day will come when a nation
> renowned in wars and victories, distinguished by the
> highest development of military order and intelligence
> and accustomed to make the heaviest sacrifice to these
> objects will voluntarily exclaim, "We will break our
> swords," and will destroy its whole military system, lock,
> stock, and barrel. Making ourselves defenceless (after
> having been the most strongly defended) from a loftiness
> of sentiment—that is the means toward genuine peace,
> which must always rest upon a pacific disposition. The
> so-called armed peace that prevails at present in all
> countries is a sign of a bellicose disposition, of a disposi-
> tion that trusts neither itself nor its neighbor, and, partly
> from hate, partly from fear, refuses to lay down its
> weapons. Better to perish than to make oneself hated and
> feared. This must some day become the supreme maxim
> of every political community.

Some Christians have glorified war and led their nations
to an anticipated conquest of the world. Thus man arose
from barbarism to dignity, they allege! "Death is the crowning of life, and how can an intelligent, free, moral creature
like man end his life more nobly than on the battlefield?"
As long as moral values are approved, there will be war!
Divine in origin, demanded by conscience, establishing justice, taught in the Bible, war is the cause of human progress!
Thus even Christians have argued.

But no intelligent Christian should any longer insist that
God is ever requiring the shedding of man's blood because

Abraham, Moses, Joshua, and David, all approved men of God, were valiant warriors, because God drowned Pharaoh's army, and because soldiers as such are not condemned in the New Testament. The proof-text employment of the Bible is unethical for both fundamentalist and pacifist. When Fundamentalism condemns pacifists for having come "in unduly large proportion . . . from the ranks of the socialists, humanists, modernists, atheists, and communists," it is publishing to the world the undoubted fact that the church has proved itself impotent with reference to the problem of war.

A critical analysis of recent American social-economic legislation makes labor and the state its initiators. Some Christians fight for it and more against it. The churches as institutions no longer control the social order. They may determine the outcome when those in favor of and those opposed to a particular measure are rather evenly divided. But any local church of stratified membership could not afford to risk its future by radical procedure. Ministers who thought their churches united on the enforcement of the prohibition amendment sometimes found themselves supported by only a hopeless minority. Direct action on matters of social-economic significance will be taken by the churches less frequently hereafter. The day of mass signing of petitions after the morning service is over. Churches will not desire to be classified as propaganda societies.

Yet all this should not prevent the various denominations from keeping abreast of today's social-economic advance nor from criticism or commendation of proposed programs. By investigating local moral and economic conditions and doing something about them, the churches might hope some day to find a revised edition of *Your City* on sale, no longer reading that church membership denotes opposition to murder, to venereal diseases, and to illegitimate births but not necessarily the promotion of the good life. "The communities with largest percentage of church members are below average in good reading, home ownership, and continuance in school and have more than their share of illiterates and child labor." Churches need to be more than passers of pious resolutions.

It will ever be the function of the churches to promote an ethical interpretation of the social order, insisting upon items like these: that society must be just to all groups and individuals, that "the unlimited exercise of the right of private ownership is socially undesirable," that child labor is a disgrace, that women need special protection in industry, that economic security is the right of everyone, that rural and city workers must learn how to co-operate, that vocational and general education for all adults desiring it shall be provided, that "unjust barriers of trade, color, creed, and race" shall be removed, that the trend toward internationalism and peace shall be encouraged. Unless the churches prefer completely to surrender their remaining influence in their own groups in the social-economic area, the curriculum of religious education must be rebuilt to provide objective handling of these subjects. The challenge is there. Will it be accepted?

Chapter Fourteen

Understanding Intercultural Relations

The problem of intercultural relations has been moved up on the agenda of the American conscience. The groups attempting to understand it are rapidly increasing. The attack upon it proceeds from many angles. It is no longer a sofa affair but a very lively, practical matter for religion, industry, human relations, the colleges, the universities, and professional life. It is inescapable, confronting American life in every village, town, and city. It is urgent. Postponement of its consideration would not be a solution but would only increase its complications. And the Charter of the United Nations demands international and social co-operation, "universal respect for, and observance of, human rights and fundamental freedoms for all without distinction as to race, sex, language, or religion." Bridges for cultural understanding are being built not only by politicians but also by science, not only in education, economics, and government but also in art and music and philosophy. Articles, pamphlets, books, bureaus, excellent bibliographies, plays in quality and in quantity, "Springfield Plans," address themselves to the interpretation of the symptoms of racialism, religious friction, social hatred, the many unfair practices with reference to minority groups, the insidious propaganda systems disturbing to intercultural good will, all types of discrimination.

This confession from Barth, Farner, and Vogt concerning Nazism may be belated but is worth recording:

Proofs are not lacking of what this regime intended and wished and we have plenty of statements on what has happened in German concentration camps since 1933. It is a fact that in the past twelve years hundreds of thousands of Germans and millions of Jews of all countries have suffered as victims of this regime. It is a fact that the Government and governing circles of those countries which are now at war with Germany found it possible *from 1933 to 1939* to treat this terrorist regime with respect and to remain inactive. It is a fact that neutral Governments have suppressed for State reasons the spreading of this news up to a short time ago, although they had abundant evidence of its truth. *It is, moreover, true that Christian circles also have neglected to make their knowledge known. It is quite natural that those who are conducting the war and the peoples of neutral countries* should today awaken to the full truth and should realize with whom and with what they have to deal. . . . He who remained indifferent before or sympathetic towards the spirit of Hitlerism at its inception has no right today to try to put the blame for these horrors on others.

From this ethical awakening should come repentance for past wrongs and greater determination to live together as good neighbors.

Enlightened religious men and women are in the vanguard and in all the ranks of the intercultural movement. But their thinking and activity ought to be carried over into their own inheritance to a greater extent. Niemoeller's *Here Stand I* was read throughout the United States. Every person regardless of religious tenets admired its heroic author for his bravery in challenging Nazism and paying the penalty in a concentration camp. After his recently reported confession of racial prejudice, this default in German Christianity has again come prominently into debate. Many who extolled the submarine officer were ignorant of this defect in character because the English translation of *Here Stand I* had suppressed the following: "We speak of the 'eternal Jew' and conjure the picture of a restless wanderer who has no home and cannot find peace. We see a highly gifted people which produces idea after idea for the benefit of the world, *but whatever it takes up becomes poisoned*, and all that it ever reaps is contempt and hatred because ever and anon the world notices the deception and avenges itself in its own way." The rest of the omitted paragraph hardly reduces this distortion of history.

In the official weekly of an American religious group noted for its emphasis upon the true faith and baptism there appeared half a dozen years back two references in successive weeks to the contemporary Jewish tragedy. In the first, after suggesting that American Jews adopt all the persecuted German Jews, the writer continues: "To the question why the Jews now and at all times have been persecuted, we should like to reply with the passage from the Bible, Matthew 27:24, 25. . . . You see the curse of the evil deed is, as the poet says, that it must continuously give birth to evil. Daniel Schubert has described the terrible result of the rejection of Christ in the poem, 'The Eternal Jew.' "

In the second reference to the present fate of the Jew, the writer continues: "We biblically oriented persons intend to think and act according to the purpose of God. We shall pray for Israel that it may interpret the present persecution according to the purpose of God. We shall pray for Israel that it may interpret the present persecution according to the divine plan and very soon express a desire to accept the Messiah [i.e. Jesus]." What infinite Christian cant and hypocrisy and effrontery!

Or consider this excerpt from a Bible history formerly very widely used in the religious training of American youth: "For eighteen hundred years has the blood of Christ been upon the Jews. Driven from Judea—without country, without home—strangers amongst strangers—hated, yet feared—have they wandered from nation to nation, bearing with them the visible signs of God's curse. Like Cain, marked with a mysterious sign, they shall continue to wander till the end of the world."

It is very regrettable that just as the intercultural movement gets under way there should be such an increased emphasis upon the Lenten season in American Protestantism. From the fourth century to the modern age, the church celebrated Good Friday as a day of prayer for the world. Today the so-called seven words from the cross are texts for the cultivation of considerable emotionalism over Calvary. Whereas the early story of the passion of Jesus was one of restraint, the celebration of it in too many Christian circles at present tends toward baroque exploitation of physical suffering. The three hours' service dates from 1732, a contribution of Lima, Peru. In 1865, England conformed; Rome had some years earlier. And now, "Veronica's Veil," "America's Passion Play," and "Golgotha" are presented for the edification of children in the United States.

Gobineau's racism has gone down to ignominious defeat by science. Peake disposed of the Nordic myth in a single sentence: "All men living at the present day, since they are all fertile *inter se*, are descended from the same group of ancestors and are the same species, *Homo Sapiens*." Haddon concluded that "race names, such as Nordic or Alpine, are merely convenient abstractions helping us to appreciate broad facts. A race type exists mainly in our own minds. There is no such thing as racial culture." There is no such thing as a pure race. Dr. Ammon of Baden "measured thousands of heads, and yet was not able to find a perfect specimen in all details. All his round-headed men were either blond, or tall, or narrow-nosed, or something else that they ought not to be." Marett of Oxford affirmed that "judged simply by his emotions, man is very much alike everywhere, from China to Peru. They are all there in germ, though different customs and grades of culture tend to bring special types of feeling to the fore." Nordic claims cover too much ground; for example, "Dante, Michael-angelo, Leonardo da Vinci, and virtually all the leading men of the Renaissance were blood Nordics"! But is this worse than an American's affirmation that the Germans lost the war of 1914 to 1918 because they had become Alpine? "The voice of blood and race" does not determine thought. Ash-ley-Montague found that race is not "a compound of physical, mental, personality and cultural traits which *determine* the behavior of the individuals inheriting this alleged compound." "Men of outstanding ability have oftenest arisen not from inbreeding within castes, but from out-breeding in the general population." In a word, race theories have sometimes been discovered to be "ideological disguisers of the dominators' and exploiters' interests."

Lest we become confused, let Edwin G. Conklin be heard: "It is generally held by scientists that all existing races of men belong to one species, *Homo sapiens*, because these races are generally fertile *inter se*. But fertility is not a safe and certain criterion of a species. Some individuals belonging to distinct species are fertile *inter se* while other individuals belonging to the same species are sterile. But, if the differences between the different races of men are not sufficiently great to warrant placing racial groups in different species, they are at least great enough to constitute sub-species." Krogman clarifies the situation still further by defining a human race as a "group more or less set apart by a certain combination of physical traits *which are inherited*." Thus, the genus is *homo*; the species, *sapiens*; the sub-species, *stocks* (Caucasian, Mongoloid, Negro); the sub-sub-species of the Caucasian: Nordic, Alpine, Mediterranean, East Baltic, and Dinaric.

Myrdal's *An American Dilemma* has been called "the most penetrating and important book on our contemporary civilization." It consists of 1483 pages devoted to the study of race relations in the United States and their international consequences. Samuel S. Wyer of Columbus, Ohio, has published a 29-page comprehensive digest of the research of the brilliant "professor in the University of Stockholm, economic adviser to the Swedish Government and member of the Swedish senate," chosen for his ability to be objective in the interpretation of the American dilemma. The following quotes from Wyer's *Digest*, it is hoped, will entice many Americans to study Myrdal's conclusions:

The "American Dilemma," referred to in the title of this book, is the ever-raging conflict between, on the one hand, the valuations preserved on the general plane which we shall call the "American Creed," where the American thinks, talks, and acts under the influence of high national and Christian precepts, and, on the other hand, the valuations on specific planes of individual and group living, where personal and local interests; economic, social, and sexual jealousies; considerations of community prestige and conformity; group prejudice against particular persons or types of people; and all sorts of miscellaneous wants, impulses, and habits dominate his outlook.

The white man's rank order of discriminations:
1. Intermarriage
2. Social equality
3. Segregation
4. Political rights
5. Equality before law
6. Economic equality.

The Negro's own rank order is just about parallel, but inverse, to that of the white man. The Negro resists least the discrimination on the ranks placed highest in the white man's evaluation and resents most any discrimination on the lowest level.

The dominant interest in rationalizing and defending the caste system can be specified in the demand that the following statements shall be held true:

1. The Negro people belongs to a separate race of mankind.
2. The Negro race has an entirely different ancestry.
3. The Negro race is inferior in as many capacities as possible.
4. The Negro race has a place in the biological hierarchy somewhere between the white man and the anthropoids.
5. The Negro race is so different both in ancestry and in characteristics that all white peoples in America, in contradistinction to the Negroes, can be considered a homogeneous race.
6. The individuals in the Negro race are comparatively similar to one another . . . are definitely more akin to one another than to any white man.

The South is also strongly religious. Not only is the nonchurch member comparatively rare, but the denominations tend to be more fundamentalist and evangelical than in the North. Although it would have to be checked by carefully collected data, my impression is that the sermons stress the Other World more often than this one and rely for a text more often on the Old Testament than on the New Testament. It would seem that the Southern white man, especially in the lower classes, goes to church more to get an emotional thrill than to get an intellectual framework into which to put his daily problems.

Both the strength and the weakness of the Negro church as a power agency for the Negro people is related to the facts that the Negro church is a segregated church and that there is astonishingly little interracial cooperation between white and Negro churches.

Southern whites usually succeed in keeping the Christian challenge of religious brotherhood off their minds. The observer feels that the very incompatibility between the uncompromising Christian creed, on the one hand, and the actual caste relations, on the other hand, is a reason why white ministers in the South keep so aloof from the race problem and why the white church in the South has generally played so inconsequential a part in changing race relations.

But viewed as an instrument of collective action to improve the Negroes' position in American society, the church has been relatively inefficient and uninfluential.

The final finding of Myrdal though challenging is not hopeless: "Not since Reconstruction has there been more reason to anticipate fundamental changes in American race relations, changes which will involve a development toward the American ideals." But this was written before the United States Senate filibuster on FEPC.

Meanwhile, the Negro the world over daily recalls the memorable words of one who went to Lambarene in equatorial Africa as a missionary (on his own), not as a pioneer of western culture or even to promote world-brotherhood *but solely to make expiation for the sins of the white man against the Negro.* Here is Albert Schweitzer's confession of sin: "A heavy guilt rests upon our culture. What have not the whites of all nations since the era of discovery done to the colored peoples! What does it signify that so many peoples where Christianity came died out and others are vanishing or at least disintegrating? Who will describe the injustices and atrocities committed by Europeans? Who would estimate what alcohol and the awful diseases we transmitted to them have done to them? If history told all that has happened between whites and blacks, many pages would be turned without reading them. A heavy guilt rests upon us. We must serve them. When we do good to them, it is not benevolence; it is expiation; it is atonement."

Biological, sociological, and religious solutions of the Jewish problem are continuously being proposed. Mixed marriages and biological assimilation turn out to be only a partial solution. For sacred traditions and marriage customs and rites interfere. Distinct differences in occupational choice may reflect the influence of the hostile social environment to which the Jewish people have been exposed through the centuries. Distinctive Jewish psychological reactions to external conditions may point to a "collective soul." The right of large numbers of persecuted and dislocated European Jews to enter Palestine in the existing emergency has been recognized and urged by President Truman. There is also the prior right under the Balfour Declaration. Britain's opportunist decision of 1939 is regrettable. Why assume that a people which has been a minority group for most of its history would not protect minority groups in any area over which it happened to rule? But there will always be an extra-Palestine Judaism entitled to life, liberty, and the pursuit of happiness. And any proposed solution of the Jewish problem which assumes that Judaism has fulfilled its mission by teaching monotheism to Christianity and Islam, and that, therefore, biological fusion must now be accompanied by social and spiritual fusion—to write more brutally, that the solution of the Jewish problem is the extinction of the Jew—would be the beginning of the end of the Charter of the United Nations. That charter does not contemplate a one-world melting pot but equal liberty for all the different peoples of the world.

Religious assimilation is not the solution of the Jewish problem. Christianity is final for Christians, Islam for Mohammedans, Hinduism for Hindus, Buddhism for Buddhists, and so on. In the one world of the future there will be more varieties of religion, not fewer. Why then should the mother of Christianity and Islam vanish? One authoritarian religion would destroy the Charter of the United Nations. Hence, religious freedom must be guaranteed to every tribe and nation the world over.

The words with which Martin Buber, in his debate with Karl Ludwig Schmidt in the pre-Hitler era, closed his apology for the right of the Jew to cherish his faith demonstrate that Judaism cannot perish:

I live near the city of Worms to which I am bound by ancestral ties. From time to time I journey thither. When I do, I always visit the Christian cathedral first. It is a visible harmony of parts, a totality, in which there is no departure from perfection. I walk around observing the cathedral with joy. Then I walk over to the Jewish cemetery. It consists of crooked, disintegrating, formless, purposeless stones. I stand in it, look up from this chaos to the majestic harmony of the cathedral. I seem to be looking up to the Church from Israel. Down here there is no form or beauty. Here are only stones and ashes under the stones. *But the ashes are here even if concealed under the stones! And here are the bodies of the people who have been turned into dust. Here they are. I have them. I do not have them as bodies upon this planet but I do possess them as forms of my personal memory into the depths of history, back to Mount Sinai itself.*

I stand there in the little Jewish cemetery near the

Christian cathedral and am united with the ashes of my fathers and thereby with the patriarchs themselves. *It is the memory of co-operation with God common to all Jews. And the perfection of Christianity cannot efface it. Nothing can destroy Israel's working with God.*

I have stood there and personally experienced all the deaths, all the ashes, all the schisms, all the silent suffering of the Jew. *But the covenant with God survives.* I lie on the ground like these stones but I survive.

The cathedral is the cathedral. The Jewish cemetery is as it is. *But we survive.*

We have seen over and over in the course of this study that the trend in the contemporary western world is toward a new religious synthesis based on science. But an historical approach to any religion destroys its claims to uniqueness and enhances also its values.

What a variety of religious experiences would be lost to the future if the religions of the world were to be fused into a single standardized institution!

The solution of intercultural relations through religious fusion is a miracle our generation will not witness and ought not to witness. Only in religious variation is there any hope for religious equality and for the separation of church and state. When at some distant future date, all the religions of the earth have been ethicized, there will result a natural religious unity of understanding based upon science and democracy.

There is another point that advocates of religious fusion might try to remember. In one co-operative world of the future the non-religious, the godless, must possess equal rights with the religious or the one-world paradise will become a one-world hell. Hence cultural and religious pluralism is the only solution of any minority problem. From the monotony of peering into the melting pot one turns with delight to listen to the international symphonic orchestra.

And support for cultural pluralism is at last coming from national minorities, labor unions, the British Council of Churches, the World's Evangelical Alliance, the Charter of the United Nations, intercultural movements, schools, churches, state legislatures, the National Conference of Christians and Jews, the Federal Council of the Churches, philosophers, historians, scientists, and men of good will in every nation.

If in American intercultural relations, most can rise from the levels of scapegoating and discrimination and prejudice and predilection to those of tolerance and respect and cooperation within the next quarter century, the millennial aeon will have dawned. Science, education, and ethical religion are uniting to promote every type of effort toward intercultural appreciation. The *ABC of Scapegoating* might well be assigned as required reading for all religious educational groups, since it not only traces prejudice to its roots but also shows how baneful all scapegoating is to democracy: "Democracy means respect for the person. Scapegoating means disrespect for the person. In the smaller and more integrated world that will follow this war, democracy and scapegoating of minority groups cannot coexist. It is for this reason that our battle against scapegoating is essentially the battle for democracy."

Chapter Fifteen

Toward a New Religious Synthesis

Life is development, the continuous adjustment between the living organism and nature. The older religious synthesis of Christendom has been dissolved by the modern environment. A new religious synthesis based on science is forming. If this means modification of religious doctrine, so be it. Religion has ever been subject to change.

The Bible is constantly quoted in defense of what has been, yet its books contain illustration after illustration of a growing faith. A revised verdict on Christianity's past has been long overdue.

Hosea revised Elijah within a century. In I and II Kings is recorded the story of the end of the house of Omri. Naboth, the Jezreelite, had a vineyard in Jezreel near the palace of King Ahab. Naboth refused to sell his vineyard to his King. Jezebel, wife of the King, intervened, lodging a charge of blasphemy and treason against Naboth. Two false witnesses sustained the accusation; King Ahab moved in.

But the Lord did not like this. Acting through his prophet, Elijah, God declared: "Hast thou killed and also taken possession? In the place where dogs licked the blood of Naboth, shall dogs lick thy blood, even thine. And of Jezebel, also spake the Lord saying, The dogs shall eat Jezebel by the rampart of Jezreel."

The Lord selected and appointed Jehu for this work of

extermination. Elisha, prophet of the Lord, sent one of his subordinates to anoint Jehu as both King and executioner. Jehu faithful to his divine directive slew Ahab and his seventy sons and all his adherents and King Ahaziah and his forty-two brothers. Jezebel, her eyes painted, her head attired, was thrown out of the palace window and the dogs consumed her.

About a century after Jehu and his blood baths, there appeared in the northern kingdom a prophet, Hosea by name. To him the word of the Lord also came: "Hosea, go, take unto thee a wife. So he went and took Gomer who bore him a son. And the Lord said unto him, 'Call his name Jezreel; for yet a little while, and I will avenge the blood of Jezreel upon the house of Jehu, and will cause to cease the kingdom of the house of Israel.' "

The holy crimes of Jehu must be expiated by the destruction of the Northern Kingdom. But those murders by Jehu were inspired—God, Elijah, and Elisha had ordered them. Yet Hosea, prophet of the same God, regarded the purge of Jehu as a series of crimes. Evidently, Hosea discriminated between the real will of God and what had been transmitted as will of God. The voice of the future was revising the verdict of the past.

Was Job in agreement with his friends regarding the meaning of pain? Is the Jesus of the synoptic gospels the Logos of the Johannine literature? Was not the gospel Jesus proclaimed concerned with the Father only? There is nothing static about the religion of the Bible. There is doubt in the Book. Those who object to the rethinking of inherited doctrine may not hide behind its statements.

The history of Christianity consists of revision after revision of earlier dogmas and rites. Baptism in the New Testament is of various types and significance but never meant the cancellation of original sin. Infant baptism was not practiced by the first-century church but became obligatory in the Syrian church in mid-fifth century. Jesus' meal with his disciples before his arrest became the last meal because of his ensuing death. Moreover, it was a simple partaking of food, a breaking of bread, and the emphasis was eschatological. There is no hint of the equations, bread equals body or cup equals blood. Augustine still favored a symbolic interpretation. Toward the end of the eighth century the eastern church decided in favor of the real presence, yet in mid-ninth century prominent western theologians were still denying it. Theophagy was an achievement of the late medieval church. The doctrine of the virgin birth of Jesus, unknown in the primitive church, later demanded the faith in, and in the nineteenth century the dogma of, the immaculate conception of his mother. The birthday of Jesus, historically unknown, was assigned to the winter equinox in the fourth century. What ceremony of the contemporary Christian churches existed in the first-century church?

Luther and Calvin revised the Catholic conclusions. John Wesley wrote that "the ape is the rough draft of man, an imperfect representation which nevertheless bears a resemblance to him, and is the last creature that serves to display the *admirable progression of the works of God.* . . ."

Let us review some recent efforts to reinterpret religious doctrines and to adapt religion to our changing world.

Observing that "science has abolished God, heaven, and hell as external to the universe and has freed us from the influence of magic, taboos, fear, and superstition," Stuart A. Courtis insisted that "religion must build her developing truths and interpretations upon scientific experimentation and generalization before she can win the loyalty of intelligent youth." The church of the future should be a "center for creative religious research, an inspirer, organizer, and integrator of scientific truth about the human aspects of religious experiences."

In *Recent Social Trends* the research on American religion made it crystal clear that ecclesiastical religion is in decline here with personal religious interest on the increase. The ethical aspects of religion receive attention; the dogmas are passed by. Between 1905 and 1930 the decline in interest in traditional Christian emphases was over 50 per cent, but open-minded religion had more support. As Whitehead insists, "the awful ultimate fact is the human being consciously alone with itself, for its own sake. Religion is what the individual does with his own solitariness. . . . It is the transition from God as void to God as enemy, and from God as enemy to God as companion."

Waterman in *Religion Faces the World Crisis,* a book which might serve as a text in the coming religious education, defines religion as "man's persistent endeavor to adjust the reality within him to the most significant realities without, for the purpose of preserving and enhancing the values of personality." There is a constant in religion. It is the relation of religion to personality. But there are also three variables in religion, namely, the increasing experience of man, the "methods and techniques of coming to terms with reality," and the social factors. Religion, then, is growth.

Ames identifies "the religious consciousness with the consciousness of the greater values of life."

For Mecklin, "religion is *primarily an emotional reaction* called out by contact, real or imaginary, with the ultimate forces of life. This reaction finds expression in ritual and symbol. When symbols have been rationalized we get creeds, doctrine, and religious philosophy. Along with this goes also a social technique consisting of forms of worship, church organization, and educational or missionary institutions, *all of which look to the preservation and propagation of this emotional attitude. . . .*"

Percy Hughes recognizes three kinds of contemporary religion—secular religion, political religions, and the religion of the churches.

Secular religion is a "consecration of the spirit to ideal ends that, without benefit of clergy, enables many persons." It "emerges from our commercial, scientific, esthetic, and moral endeavors."

A political religion is one that "engages the hearts of men so utterly that beside it, church-fostered religions seem as a rule rather pallid affairs." A political religion may be Fascist or democratic. It may be Fuehrer-worship, emperor-worship, or worship of the democratic ideal.

What, now, is the religion of the churches (not merely Christian churches but non-Christian churches as well)? What is a church historically viewed? The philosopher answers that a church is "an institution devoted to maintaining an autotelic, autonomous tradition of spiritual nurture." When churches lean toward politics or "cling to residues of theocratic tradition for their authority" they are despised. They cannot speak authoritatively with regard to philosophy, politics, science, or history without "systematically falsifying cosmic and historic data." The function of all the churches, Christian and non-Christian, is to "maintain and develop a tradition of observances through which may be transmitted the spirit or attitude in and toward life, of men and women who have seemed in some special way in supreme degree masters of life." Churches may not resort to myth and symbol unless "some genuinely religious function" is hindered by adherence to fact. "Spiritual insight" is not "competent to pass on matters of morals and government, of cosmic order and of historic fact." Churches in all the religions of the world have inspirational value. This apology for the religion of the churches is a complete reconstruction of the churches' own claims and faith, granting them primarily societal significance.

This trend toward the sociological interpretation of religion now more than a century old was popularized by Durkheim's thesis that "the reality which is the universal and permanent objective cause of the sensations out of which religious experience is made, is society." "The real function of religion is not to make us think, to enrich our knowledge, nor to add to the conceptions which we owe to science . . . but rather to make us act, to aid us to live. . . . Nearly all the great social institutions have been born in religion. . . . If religion has given birth to all that is essential in society, it is because the idea of society is the soul of religion."

Dimock describes religion as "a complex of ideas, attitudes, habits, customs, and practices developed by a group as it adjusts itself to its total environment, social and natural, in the endeavor to achieve those values and satisfactions which are considered most worthful." Haydon puts it all into a single sentence: "Religion is the cooperative quest for a completely satisfying life." Sellars agrees: "Religion is the spirit and quality of human living . . . the strategy of human life in the face of destiny . . . the self-conscious human life functioning in the face of its problems. . . . A humanist religion cannot be a passive thing; it must cry out the command for the cooperative creation of the good life upon the earth." So does Max Otto: "It was mankind that brought purpose and choice into the world, not purpose and choice that brought mankind." According to Dietrich, humanism involves: "1. Belief in the supreme worth of human life and of man; 2. The effort to understand human experience by means of human inquiry; 3. The effort to enrich human experience to the utmost capacity of man and of his environment; 4. The acceptance of responsibility for the conditions of human life and the entire reliance upon human effort for their improvement."

Charles Morris in *Paths of Life* daringly constructs a new religious synthesis in terms of the components of human personality. These are the *dionysian*, acceptance of and reliance on the world, release and indulgence of existing desires, enjoyment; the *promethean*, creative "active tendencies to manipulate and remake the world"; the *buddhistic*, restraint, self-control, regulation of desires, detachment, solitude, meditation. The proportion of each component in a path of life determines its character. In the course of human history six paths have plainly appeared. The Buddhist with dionysian and promethean elements has explored one path. The other five paths have been the Dionysian, the Promethean, the Apollonian, the Christian, and the Mohammedan. The Christian ratio is dionysian, two; promethean, one; buddhistic, three. The Christian path has been very winding and adaptable. Its mythology, theology, and philosophy are derived. It has been a religion of redemption, of scorn of science and technology, of revelation, of inspired Book, of authoritarian dicta. But it also perpetuates the "humanistic traditions of Greece." "The Catholic Church has—perhaps fatally—rested its case on Aquinas." Each of the six paths of life has failed to be completely satisfying to man. Hence a seventh path of life already trodden by some is proposed as the solution of man's problem. It is built on a balance of the dionysian, promethean, and buddhistic components of human personality. It is called the Maitreyan way and is neither indifference nor attachment, is more than affirmation or negation, in harmony with science, a syncretism of the values in the six other paths of life.

Horace Kallen in *Why Religion* fascinatingly describes how the essential experience of the mystic is that of freedom, liberating him from confinement within the conventional religious patterns and the institution's demands, permitting him to experience religion in art, science, godlessness, challenging him at times to reject existing ideas and institutions. This kind of religion is indestructible; at least, it fits into that kind of adaptation of religion to life that we have advocated.

But, during secularization of an inherited religion, there

is always a contraction of its functions. Divination, exorcism, and prophecy are assigned to astrologer, palmist, fortune teller, and, we might add, prophet and apocalyptist Long who had an alibi for the failure of the Lord to return at 10:33 A.M., September 21, 1945. The health officer now arranges for the quarantine, the weather bureau predicts coming temperature and rainfall, and irrigation takes care of crops—all these were religious functions in the age of faith. The symbolism of the medieval period appears in the initiation services of American lodges. The dance, originally religious and magical, first is secularized, then opposed by the churches, and, finally, made religious again by being held in a church gymnasium. Theology at first repudiates science, then compromises with it, and at last remembers that it always believed that way, finding "proof" in the Bible or substituting teleology for determinism and free will for mutation. Even within the Jehovah's Witnesses' cult, city dwellers and factory workers are more liberal than the rural members. The faith of the fathers possibly survives in greater quantity among village fundamentalists than city modernists. Is not socialism the City of God for socialists and capitalism the City of This World? A recent Pope observed in *Mit brennender Sorge*, 1937, that Nazism had taken over such major words of the Christian vocabulary as revelation, faith, immortality, cross, humility, and grace and given them National Socialistic connotation.

Hence, by cultural advance, transfer, compromise, the medieval religious synthesis has become so attenuated for countless contemporary intellectuals that only the problem of death remains for solution.

Helen Wodehouse in *One Kind of Religion* moves away from the mythology of traditional Christianity to a personal religion in agreement with intellectual honesty as God becomes "the sum or the substance of all good."

In his "Oceanic Christianity," Vergilius Ferm writes:

Thus, it seems to me that evil will never be overcome. Nor, curiously enough, ought it to be. The only other alternative would be neutrality (in which there would be neither good nor bad) or else a state or condition of purposelessness or rest (the worst kind of hell). The really good person is the one who has many frustrations to his purposes of self-realization and who emerges out of the valley of shadows. He is never without opposition or pain. . . . God can no more save a man from evil than he can save himself from it. Nor should he. To do so, I repeat, would be to annihilate the values which make life meaningful and rich. Our soteriology needs reinspection in the light of all this. But so many people still think that to speculate on soteriological theory is to toy with the one basic essential to the Christian religion, *forgetting that all our theories of salvation are ideologies of men who reflect the limitations of their age and perspective.**

A few of the more recent types of religious thought have thus been presented—too concisely and inadequately, to be sure. They must suffice to indicate some of the content of the new religious synthesis slowly emerging in the western world. Whichever of these patterns one examines, the absence of the dogmatic symbols of Christendom, of the traditional emphases upon revelation, inspiration of the Bible, and authority is too conspicuous to be missed. The pressures urging these writers on come from the scientific spirit and the democratic faith. Not one takes refuge in symbolism or in faith or "the given" when confronted with the facts of modern life. The old appeal to something fixed or given has vanished. Gone are absolutistic claims and deliverances. Oracles and prophecy have yielded to research and reason. The findings of the laboratory and of history are accepted. All make use of the rich deposit of experience in the religious literatures of the world to ascertain how

* *The Crozer Quarterly,* January, 1946.

other persons found their way through the maze called life.
For it would be unscientific not to include this material
which also represents human achievement. Unless one is
familiar with the great cultures of the world, he will not be
able to understand the problems which will face the United
Nations.

There is a new kind of reverence here, a feeling of how
fragmentary the best research is. Here is the forward look.
Professor Arthur E. Murphy in another connection mod-
estly summarizes the mood of those who are trying to for-
mulate the coming religious synthesis: "We do not know
all the answers yet, being in this respect less fortunate than
some of the traditionalists, and even when we get them,
there will be still more questions. But we have learned
enough, from tradition and experience, to be reasonably
assured that in the process of finding answers to such problems there is enough to learn and achieve, to keep both us
and our students very profitably at work and to further, in
ways beyond our present calculation, the actualization of
those spiritual values in which the enterprise of human
understanding finds its appropriate and adequate fulfil-
ment."

To measure the newer interpretation of religion in terms
of progress, recall Bishop Butler's "religion is a belief in
one God or creator and moral governor of the world and
in a future state of retribution," or Tylor's "religion is the
belief in Spiritual Beings," or "religion is an invention of
priests," or "religion is an anaesthetic."

Will the growth of the new religious synthesis continue in
the United States, which has recently become the battle-
ground of the European orthodoxies? The dissolution of
the ancient partnership between the culture of Europe and
Christianity during the twentieth century has greatly weakened and made ineffective dogmatic religion over there. It
seeks to regain its lost prestige and power here. Can Ameri-

can dogmatic religion rejuvenated by the remnants of European dogmatic theology transplanted to these shores hope to control or at least to condition and circumscribe the growth of democratic religion among us? Or are the scientific spirit and the democratic faith now such healthy plants and so antithetical to monopolistic religious authoritarianism and European-American religious cartels as to be able to resist such infection? Will religious freedom, growth, variation, creativeness, and understanding succumb to tradition, anathema, conformity, fear, "the justificational view," and scholastic sterility? Not if the tragedy of Christendom is recalled! Not if the forces of progress advance to the attack and employ their moral values and ideals to promote the good life. Let no charge of "activism" make them afraid.

European Christianity, seeking the protection of the state and remaining silent and submissive and obedient during the terrible years of Hitler, cannot escape its burden of guilt. It looked toward the past too long. The tradition it sought to defend was not "revelation" but the product of the reflection of the fathers much less informed than their sons! Too often tradition on examination contradicts the traditionalists. For four centuries the churches have known that I John 5:7 originated centuries after I John was composed. When it is employed as a proof text of the doctrine of the trinity, the procedure is not only intellectually dishonest but also stupid. In the twentieth century one can no longer deny that Psalm 104 and the Egyptian Akhnaton's hymn to the Sun contain parallels. Gregorian chants and chorals have eastern equivalents. The Golden Rule is not unique in Christian literature. Christianity must face the question of loss of uniqueness eventually. Why not now?

Living in a one-world environment should more than offset the invasion of European orthodoxy, which failed so miserably over there, into these parts. No missionary a few years hence will pompously read Acts 4:25 to the Chinese.

The formulation of a new religious synthesis of an inclusive pattern based on science cannot be avoided by religious education. For "no other thought area shows as much intellectual dishonesty as is found in our religion thinking, which is many years behind our science thinking." The destructive use of the discoveries of science can be prevented only by an ethical religion catch-up. If those beyond the churches exhibit a finer quality of ethical interpretation of life than those within, will not more Americans ask with Percy Hughes, "Indeed, what genuine religious need of man is there that churches may meet that may not better be met by secular schools?"

Summing up, the religious synthesis inherited from Christendom has been undermined by the powers of the modern age. Protestantism by its discrediting of the authority of the papacy and its emphasis upon individualism initiated secularization but in turn found itself a prisoner within its supernatural confessionalism and its supernaturally inspired Book. Science beginning in rather naive fashion ridiculed ascent to heaven and descent to hell by transforming a pancake earth into a constantly rotating and revolving tiny baseball. Thereupon fiat-creation surrendered to process view. "Soul" was redefined. "Original sin and guilt" became theological fiction. The historical interpretation of the Bible made it a series of human documents composed by many men in the course of many centuries. The history of religions uncovered how rites and ceremonies, legends and myths, theogonies and cosmologies, priesthoods, and creeds and sacred canons actually originated and expanded. The exact story of worship of animals, ghosts, ancestors, the king, fertility, and so on got into the record. So did human sacrifice and sexual orgies, everlasting torture, everlasting sex, the extirpation of the heretic. During the Power Age, roughly since about 1790, a new religious synthesis has been emerging.

Five principal trends in religion are recognizable today within American life, not to mention the legion of minor interpretations: 1. The defenders of the inherited synthesis in its Catholic and orthodox Protestant patterns. 2. The rejectors of all religions by definition. Religion must mean "recognition on the part of man of some unseen higher power as having control of his destiny and as being entitled to obedience, reverence, and worship." But since science has set aside supernaturalism, all religions and religion must be abandoned. 3. The groups who can no longer ridicule or deny the "facts" of scientific research and seek to enter into compromise with modern social theories and knowledge while retaining sufficient "truth" from the earlier religious synthesis to enable them honestly to continue in active support of the churches as institutions. 4. The vast majority of Americans who are individually members of every kind of religious group or no group but whose primary religion is commitment to the ideals of the American way of life. Catholic, Protestant, sectist, cultist, atheist, cultured, ignorant, business man, worker believe in democracy. 5. The fifth group, represented by some members of the orthodox churches and by people of every level of culture in American life beyond the churches. It is a cross-section of church-attendant and non-attendant. Its varieties are endless. It represents a break, major or minor, with the inherited religious synthesis. It accepts both democracy and the scientific spirit. It does not believe in the traditional heritage. It desires to move beyond the phase of compromise. It favors a religious interpretation separated from inherited dogmas— a de novo point of view based upon what has occurred since 1647. It refuses to consolidate its views in a creed because it expects to grow and also because an emphasis upon intellectual content cannot do justice to the social implications of its attitudes.

With apologies to John Dewey, the "common faith" which is emerging in so many fragmentary ways in the United States today may be viewed as the acquisition of better perspective in the interpretation of the religious quality in human nature. An activity is religious in quality when "convinced of its general and enduring value" one risks personal loss and engages in it in support of an ideal. The seat of authority is now in the controlled reflection which follows observation, experimentation, analysis. Justice, affection, intellectual integrity, and such values have an inherent authority. The optimism of institutional religion which changes sins like scarlet into whiteness of wool, which lets man separate from his original sin in the rite of baptism, is bleached into a new optimism of making capable man take the responsibility for advancing the good life instead of accepting Hitler as "put there by God." Human relations instead of being tainted by an inherited corrupt nature become "charged with values that are religious in function." And thus the new synthesis seems to approve of the ethical quadrilateral of Jesus: purity, love, humility, and heroism. With humanity and human relations by nature not evil and the good life as objective, the new synthesis should do much more for international good will than the annals of Christendom relate. For there can be peace on this earth only among men of good will. The new religious synthesis makes possible one-world religious co-operation on equal terms.

Waterman in *Religion Faces the World Crisis* states the alternative: "Organized religion if it is not to become a negligible quantity . . . must make the goal of ethical religion its main task. Sectarianism has outlived its usefulness. In the establishment of justice and good will among men . . . there can be no theological, sectarian, or ritualistic distinctions."